Jerry Snyder's GUITAR SCHOOL

Contents

Cover photos: Classical Guitar by Richard Bruné
Martin D-28 courtesy of the Martin Guitar Company
Fender Stratocaster courtesy of Fender Musical Instruments, Inc.

THE GUITAR CLASS

Background

It has only been in the last thirty years that guitar instruction has made its way into the school music curriculum. Organized guitar classes first appeared in the late 60's. At that time, very few colleges and universities offered any instruction on the guitar. Music educators had to scramble to obtain the skills and information needed to organize and teach the guitar class.

As music educators, we are continually challenged to learn and update our skills and knowledge. Our job responsibilities often require that we teach in areas in which we have not been adequately trained. We start our careers and realize that we need more information on how to teach voice and choir, on how to teach strings and an orchestra, on how to teach the jazz ensemble, on how to teach the band. As band directors we might find ourselves in charge of an orchestra program. We attend conferences, take classes, study privately, go to workshops, ask our friends for help, bring in clinicians — whatever it takes to gain the knowledge we need. Can a non-guitarist teach a guitar class? You bet they can — and do.

Teacher Preparation and Class Size

Music education majors have traditionally been required to enroll in so-called "technique of teaching" courses in band and orchestra instruments. Exposure to the guitar is sometimes included but most often it is ignored. The minimal requirements of these technique courses are:

- An understanding of the pedagogy of the instrument
- Knowledge of basic adjustment, maintenance and care
- The ability to demonstrate correct playing positions
- Some knowledge of the repertoire

The *Teacher's Guide* assumes no past experience with the guitar. It is a guide designed for the music teacher who has little or no experience with the guitar or with teaching the guitar class. While you can learn along with your students, it is advisable to take some guitar lessons to strengthen your knowledge of basic right and left hand playing techniques. For experienced guitar teachers, the *Teacher's Guide* offers many valuable suggestions, teaching strategies and supplemental materials based on the author's thirty years of experience in teaching and writing materials for the guitar class.

The guitar class should be an elective class with a maximum enrollment of 25 to 30 students. In a high school, it most often meets every day for a semester or for the school year. It attracts a heterogeneous group of students.

Facilities and Equipment

Many of the classes are taught in the band room where music stands are available. The following items are very helpful in teaching the class:

- a good capable sound system
- storage for guitars and supplemental music library
- a VCR and TV monitor
- practice rooms or a small ensemble room
- a piano
- school amplifiers
- a chalk board or marker board
- a PA system and microphones for "showcase" performances

Selecting a Guitar

In most schools, the students are required to provide their own guitar. I recommend acoustic nylon or steel string guitars, but it is okay to allow electric guitars as well (no amps except in practice rooms or for performances). There is no substitute for a quality guitar purchased from a dealer that will stand behind its product. A poorly set up guitar with high action is difficult to play and will discourage the student.

Nylon Strings

The nylon string guitar (classical) is an excellent choice for the beginner. There is less tension on the strings than on the steel string guitar, making the strings easier to depress. A distinguishing characteristic of the nylon string guitar is its open peg box. The tone quality is dark, mellow and somewhat delicate. Do not put steel strings on this guitar.

Steel Strings

There are about a hundred pounds more pressure on the neck of a steel string guitar. An easy to play steel string guitar will be slightly more expensive than a nylon string guitar. Light gauge strings make this guitar easy to play for beginners. The neck is fairly narrow and the tone is bright, brassy and forceful.

Electric Guitars

Entry-level student electric guitars have become more affordable. That is one reason beginning students will show up with this type of guitar. While I allow this type of guitar in the class, I don't allow it to be amplified. It is too distracting for the rest of the class. The use of amplification should be limited to practice rooms (if available) and performances.

Electric Bass

There are students who will want to join the guitar class on electric bass. I have had at least two or three bass students in all of my past guitar classes. I have used my *Bass Today* method, the companion bass method to *Guitar Today*, to teach these students how to read music. This method could be used with *Guitar School*. When it comes to playing songs and chord progressions, the bass players learn to respond to chord names by first playing roots, then roots and fifths and eventually a variety of riffs, licks, and styles. When I drill chords, review songs, or play ensembles, I often have one of the bass players "plug in" to the amplifier so they can contribute to the overall sound of our ensemble.

Your guitar students will also enjoy learning something about the bass. The four strings of the bass are tuned exactly like the 3rd, 4th, 5th and 6th strings of the guitar except they are tuned an octave lower and they read in the bass clef. Don't be hesitant to add bass students to the class. It works very well and may produce a bass player for your jazz ensemble. It did that for me.

Pickstyle or Fingerstyle

I recommend that you include both types of right hand playing techniques. The *Guitar School* method and guide include explanations and material for both styles. My approach has been to require all students to learn both fingerstyle and pickstyle techniques. On a few occasions, I have introduced pickstyle techniques but made them optional for students who expressed a serious interest in the classical guitar repertoire.

Organizing for Instruction

The *Course of Study, Units of Study, Lesson Plans* and *Supplemental Material* included in this *Teacher's Guide* provide you with the organization needed for teaching the guitar class. Here are some procedures that are useful in the guitar class:

- Develop a tuning procedure (see Unit I, Lesson Six)
- Drill strum or fingerstyle arpeggios on open strings
- Teach rhythm and duration on open strings or by having the students tap on the back of their guitar (they become drum students)
- Simplify the presentation of new material by breaking it down into smaller parts that can be drilled separately
- Create guitar ensembles out of the songs; have students create bass and harmony parts
- Develop *readiness* in the students by preparing them for new skills and techniques prior to the time they have to read them out of a book or off the printed page (details in the lesson plans)

- Demand good playing posture and playing technique
- Circulate around the room and give lots of individual help
- Invite the students to bring and discuss their favorite recording
- Utilize large group, small group and individual presentation of material where appropriate
- Focus student practice time on specific assignments
- Teach the students how to practice
- Differentiate instruction in order to reach all of the students
- Closely monitor progress and set deadlines

Readiness

To adequately prepare students for various skills, it is useful to present rote or written drills as preparation exercises. These drills should focus solely on the new skill being introduced. The book, lesson plans and supplemental materials provide many suggestions on how to develop *readiness* in the students in regards to chord playing, strums, note reading, etc. Students need to be prepared for skills so that they will be **ready** when you reach various parts of the book. Too often we involve students in the confusion of musical signs and symbols before they have developed basic tone production technique. For example, before you get to the part of the book that presents fingerstyle techniques, introduce the basic hand position along with a few drills to help develop the plucking and arpeggio techniques. Pass out the *Tabsheets* to provide some drills. When you present things in this manner, you can focus on the technique and the sound being produced.

Differentiating Instruction

Perhaps you've noticed that for any curriculum you teach, there seems to be at least three levels of student readiness in your classes: students who are **not ready** for the curriculum; students who are **ready**; and students who may be **ready to go beyond**. We often aim for the students in the middle and hope that the struggling students will somehow catch up and that the more advanced students won't become too bored.

Your day-to-day observation of student progress and the *Student Survey* will help you identify the three groups of students. Differentiate the core curriculum in the guitar class so that it simultaneously serves the readiness levels of all three groups with greater equity. For example:

Struggling students who are not ready for the curriculum:
- Let them play simplified chords in the beginning
- Keep right hand accompaniment patterns simple until they have learned the chords
- Provide more time to pass achievement standards
- Assign a student tutor to them
- Provide them with more individual instruction
- For a while, allow them to write the names under the notes in notation assignments
- Use tablature to aid them in learning how to read standard music notation

Students ready to go beyond the curriculum:
- Have students who already know a few chords begin to study right hand techniques
- Allow these students to work ahead in the book
- Assign these students the *challenge* sections in the book
- Have supplemental song and method books available
- Provide theory notebooks for individual study
- Use these as mentors and aids for the struggling students
- Encourage original composition and improvisation
- Provide them with performance opportunities in class or at assemblies

Students who are ready for the curriculum:
- In general, these students are motivated and adequately challenged by the curriculum

Vocal Instruction

When guitar classes appeared in the curriculum in the late 60's, much of the focus was on learning chord accompaniment on the guitar in order to sing and perform all of the popular songs of the time (Dylan, Baez, Campbell, Mitchell, Beatles). Most of the guitar classes up through the 70's included vocal instruction and singing as part of their curriculum. In the mid 80's and early 90's, singing in the guitar class gave way to taking a more instrumental approach. Today's students seem to have a more eclectic approach. They have discovered a wide variety of performers and song styles through MTV, VH-1, the internet, and CD recordings. The interest and willingness to sing in the guitar class seems to have come back.

If you include vocal instruction in the guitar class, don't expect the students to be able to sing while playing the guitar. Develop their singing and guitar skills separately. Beginning students or inexperienced singers can't do two things at once. Begin with ear training and matching pitch. Work toward helping students discover their vocal range and register. Provide performance opportunities for the students who are able to sing . These "ice breaker" performances will encourage more students to take the plunge. As part of the vocal experience, students should:

- Discover their range and register
- Learn to sing on pitch with good breathe control and projection
- Sing a solo while playing an accompaniment on the guitar
- Learn to recognize and sing basic intervals within an octave
- Learn how to make up a harmony part

Quizzes

In addition to the *Worksheets* and Unit Tests, give frequent quizzes at the beginning of the period on specific items, such as: names of the strings on the guitar; notes in the musical alphabet and indication of where the half steps occur; have them write the counting under a short notation exercise (copy it from the board); have them name the principal chords in the Keys of D and G; provide them with a fingerboard grid and have them put in the names of the natural notes in 1st position. These periodic quizzes enable you to monitor student progress and understanding.

THE ELEMENTS OF MUSIC

Because the guitar class is a hands-on type of music class, you can develop the following concepts regarding the structure of music *as the students experience them.*

Rhythm is the basic element in our world. It can be observed in the heartbeat, the process of breathing, the alternating of day and night, the ebb and flow of the tides, and the patterns of the seasons. In music, rhythm is the most fundamental and basic element. Rhythm can be completely separated from the elements of melody and harmony. Rhythm can be described as an arrangement of long and short sounds that are organized into patterns of accented and unaccented pulses. There are several characteristics of rhythm that can be examined separately:

- *Pulse* (steady beat, irregular beat, obscured beat, gradually or suddenly changing beat)
- *Meter* (pulse is organized into groups of twos, threes, or larger units by accenting the first beat of each group)
- *Tempo* (gradual and sudden changes of the pulse and speed affect the mood and intensity of music)
- *Quality of movement* (smooth, flowing, jagged, detached)

Melody (line, a tune, a theme) in music is a series of consecutive tones (pitches) usually varying in pitch and duration and organized into a musical idea. The combination of rhythm and pitch results in melodic idea. Melody is the horizontal aspect of music. Tension and release are vital elements in creating melodic interest. A melody needs high points *(tension)* and relaxing points *(release)* to achieve musical impact. Characteristics that can be examined separately are:

- *Line* (horizontal succession of musical tones or pitches)
- *Contour* (rising, falling, leaps, skips)
- *Range* (the distance between the highest and lowest tone)
- *Register* (the relative highness or lowness of the collective tones of a melody)
- *Tonality* (based on a scale, key)

Harmony is present in many aspects of life and art. Synonyms might be: order, regularity, balance, agreement, peacefulness, friendliness. In music, harmony is the simultaneous sounding of two or more tones. A reference to harmony may be made in terms of either *chords* (the vertical relationship of tones) or, in terms of *counterpoint* (where there is also a vertical relationship present which comes from the combining of melodies). Several characteristics of harmony can be examined separately:

- *Chords* (consonant and dissonant)
- *Texture* (monophonic, homophonic, polyphonic)
- *Cadences* (arrival, emphasis, final ending)
- *Tonal center* (key, home base, related to a scale)

Tone color compares to color in art. In music, it refers to the distinctive quality of a tone produced by a particular medium of musical production: voice, instrument, or electronic device. Characteristics that can be examined separately are:

- *Quality of sound* (light-dark, warm-cool, thick-thin, brilliant-dull)
- *Amount of sound* (number playing)
- *Strength of sound* (dynamics, loudness-softness)
- *Timbre* (tone quality of the voice and various instruments

Form is the structure and design of music. It is the result of the combining of all of the elements of music. Satisfactory form in music can be achieved with a balance of *unity* and *variety*. Three principles used in composing music are:

- *Repetition* (the presentation of the same musical material which contributes to unity)
- *Contrast* (presentation of different musical material adds variety and interest)
- *Variation* (a process in which some of the musical elements remain the same while others are more or less changed)

National Standards for Arts Education

Guitar School addresses the nine content standards in music — Goals 2000: Educate America Act — as follows:

1. Content Standard: *Singing alone and with others, a varied repertoire of music.* There is a lot of opportunity in the guitar class to include singing. Vocal instruction should be presented separately before attempting to play the guitar while singing. *Proficient:* learn to match pitch, sing intervals and discover vocal range and register; sing in class, on pitch with good breath control and projection; sing in class while playing a simple guitar accompaniment. *Advanced:* sing a song alone for the teacher while playing an accompaniment on the guitar; sing a song alone for the class with guitar accompaniment; learn to sing a harmony part.

2. Content Standard: *Performing on instruments, alone and with others, a varied repertoire of music.* The guitar class provides detailed instruction in the performance of a wide variety of music representing diverse genres and cultures. *Proficient:* perform chord progressions and accompaniment patterns; perform in class, alone and in small and large ensembles; perform a varied repertoire of music that represents diverse genres and styles. *Advanced:* performing a guitar solo for the class; performing in an ensemble with one student to a part.

3. Content Standard: *Improvising melodies, variations, and accompaniments. Proficient:* playing by ear; creating original accompaniments to songs; learning how to improvise a simple solo from the minor pentatonic scale. *Advanced:* creating an improvised solo over the G minor, A minor and E minor pentatonic scales, in a blues, jazz and rock style.

4. Content Standard: *Composing and arranging music within specified guidelines. Proficient:* learning to compose music over a given chord progression; learning to create a chord progression to a given melody; arranging music for a guitar ensemble. *Advanced:* composing a song that includes lyrics and accompaniment; arranging the song for performance with voice, guitars and bass.

5. Content Standard: *Reading and notating music.* The development of music reading skills exists throughout the method. *Proficient:* learn to read music in first position on the guitar; learn to read and notate standard music notation, tablature and chord frames, performing songs, and exercises in the method; complete theory worksheets and unit test on music fundamentals. *Advanced:* learn to read music on the guitar in 3rd and 5th position; learn to read and play level 1–3 classical guitar pieces; write a classical guitar study.

6. Content Standard: *Listening to, analyzing, and describing music.* Included in the method is a recommended listening list that covers a wide variety of styles. The method CD provides an awareness of style — folk, rock, jazz, Latin, blues. Teachers will have many opportunities to make students aware of the elements of music and style. *Proficient:* listen to specific styles of music and learn to describe and analyze the use of the elements of music; notice repetition, contrast and variation in the design and structure of the music. *Advanced:* comparing ways in which the elements of music are used in various styles.

7. Content Standard: *Evaluating music and music performances.* Ample opportunity exists for students to hear and evaluate performance. *Proficient:* develop listening skills; develop a criteria for making informed evaluations; have models and examples for comparison. *Advanced:* being able to describe the aesthetic qualities of the music; being able to describe the feelings and emotions evoked by a composition.

8. Content Standard: *Understanding relationships between music, the other arts and disciplines outside the arts. Proficient:* compare the characteristics of two arts in the same historic period or style; identify and explain the ways in which the principles of other subjects taught in school are interrelated to those of music. *Advanced:* compare the use of the elements and organizational principles among the arts in various historical periods and in different cultures.

9. Content Standard: *Understanding music in relation to history and culture.* The guitar is said to be the most popular musical instrument. It has adapted well to many styles of music and diverse cultures. A sampling of the guitar repertoire, especially as an accompaniment instrument to songs, can reveal much about a culture and its history. Folk songs of many countries are included in the method. *Proficient:* identify examples of music by style and or by historical period; describe the distinguishing characteristics of various music genres. *Advanced:* describe and identify various roles that musicians play in a culture; describe their activities and contributions.

Guitar School suggests playing tests throughout the lesson plans. All of the students need to successfully complete the *Proficient* Achievement Standards. The *Advanced* Achievement Standards will challenge those students who are ready to go beyond the curriculum.

Proficient Achievement Standards

1. D-G-A7-D chord progression. Play four beats on each chord with Basic Strum No. 1.
2. Play *Mist* (p. 67).
3. Play *Chelsie* (p. 68).
4. Play *Easy Rock* (p. 70).
5. G-C-D-G chord progression. Play eight beats on each chord with the Bass/Chord Strum.
6. Play *Prelude* (p. 72).
7. D-G-A7-D-G-C-D7-G chord progression. Play four beats on each chord.
8. Play ex. 29 with a Double Bass/Chord Strum (p. 25).
9. Play *Peaceful Feeling* (p. 75).
10. Play *G Scale Study* (p. 77).
11. Play *8-Bar Blues* (p. 30), ex. 42.
12. E-A-B7-E-Em-Am-B7-Em chord progression. Play four beats on each chord.
13. Play *Spanish Song* (p. 80).
14. Play *Celebrate* (p. 83).
15. Play *Walking the Bass* (p. 39) ex. 61.
16. Play the I-IV-V7-I in the Keys of D, G, A, E and the i-iv-V7-i in Am and Em. Play the Bass/Chord Strum.
17. Play *Classical Study* (p. 87).
18. Play the fingerstyle accompaniment patterns, ex. 2–10, from *Tabsheet #1*. Use any chord except Em.
19. Play *Groovin'* (p. 89).
20. Play ex. 79 (p. 49).
21. Play ex. 85 (p. 51).
22. Play *House of the Rising Sun* (p. 91) or *Solo* (p. 94).
23. Play a Bass/Strum/Fifth/Strum pattern on all chords in the Keys of D, G, A, E, C, Am and Em.

Advanced Achievement Standards

1. Improvise a solo on the G minor pentatonic scale.
2. Improvise a solo on the A minor pentatonic scale.
3. Improvise a solo on the E minor pentatonic scale.
4. Play *Andante* from *Notesheet #4*.
5. Play the *Am Study* from *Notesheet #5*.
6. Play *Rocking the Blues* from *Notesheet #7*.
7. Play *Spanish Theme* from *Notesheet #8*.
8. Play the *Moveable G* and *C Scales* in eighth notes.

Listening Activities

The recordings of the following artists represent a wide variety of styles.

Blues (electric): Elvin Bishop, Mike Bloomfield, Roy Bucanan, Eric Clapton, Robert Cray, Albert King, Buddy Guy, B. B. King, Johnny Lang, Bonnie Raitt, Stevie Ray Vaughn, T. Bone Walker, Muddy Waters (acoustic): Corey Harris, Robert Johnson, Keb' Mo'

Classical: Julian Bream, Elliot Fisk, Oscar Ghiglia, Sharon Isbin, Christopher Parkening, Andres Segovia, Scott Tennant, John Williams

Contemporary Acoustic: William Ackerman, Alex de Grassi, John Fahey, Stephen Grossman, Michael Hedges, Leo Kottke, Adrian Legg, Martin Simpson

Country: Chet Atkins, Roy Clark, Willie Nelson, Jerry Reed, Merle Travis, Doc Watson

Flamenco: Paco de Lucia, Carlos Montoya, Manitas de Plata, Sabicas, Juan Serrano

Folk/Rock: The Byrds, Bob Dylan, Crosby, Stills and Nash, Simon and Garfunkel, Buffalo Springfield

Fusion: Larry Carlton, Larry Coryell, Al DiMeola, Allan Holdsworth, John McLaughlin, Lee Ritenour

International: Keola Beamer (*slack key*), Antonio Carlos Jobim (*bossa nova*), Bob Marley (*reggae*), Jorge Morel (*latin*), Ernest Ranglin (*ska*)

Jazz (*electric*): John Abercrombie, George Benson, Kenny Burrell, Charlie Christian, Freddie Green, Herb Ellis, Tal Farlow, Stanley Jordan, Barney Kessell, Pat Martino, Pat Metheny, Wes Montgomery, Joe Pass, Django Reinhart, Johnny Smith (*nylon*): Laurendo Almeida, Charlie Byrd, Earl Klugh, Bola Sete

Popular: Glen Campbell, Roy Clark, John Denver, Jose Feliciano, Tony Mottola, Les Paul, Mason Williams

Traditional Folk: Joan Baez, Leadbelly, Pete Seeger, Doc Watson, Weavers

Rock: The Beatles, Jeff Beck, Chuck Berry, Eric Clapton, Jimi Hendrix, Eric Johnson, Yngwie Malmsteen, Brian May, Jimmy Page, Joe Perry, Keith Richard, Joe Satriani, Pete Townsend, Eddie Van Halen, Steve Vai, Angus Young, Neil Young

Websites

There are several websites that provide additional material and information about the guitar and supplementary materials. The Yahoo Search Engine Guitar Links currently lists 142 links. Some good links to get you started are:

- MENC/GAMA/NAMM website at http://guitarweb.music.duq.edu/gen
- On Line Archive of Guitar Links

COURSE DESCRIPTION

This is an elective course offering beginning instruction on the guitar. It covers open chords, power chords, moveable chords, accompaniment techniques and a variety of playing techniques and styles including both the pickstyle and finger-style approaches to the guitar. The course also includes music fundamentals, theory, songs, performing, listening, composing, improvising, analyzing and learning how to read standard music notation and tablature.

Goals

- To learn how to play chords, accompaniment and melodies on the guitar
- To learn how to read music notation, chord frames and tablature
- To develop an understanding of music fundamentals and theory
- To learn how to perform, write and create music
- To develop the ability to analyze, describe and listen to music
- To develop the ability to match pitch and sing on pitch
- To develop an understanding of music in relation to history and culture

Guitar Technique

Chords
- Principal chords -in first position in the Keys of D, G, A, E, Em, Am and C
- Secondary chords — ii, iii and vi
- Embellished chords — major and minor 6ths, major and minor 7ths, add9
- Altered chords — suspended, minor #7th, dominant 7th♭9
- Moveable chords -major, minor, 6th, 7th and dominant 9th type chords

Accompaniment
- Pickstyle strums — various pop, blues, ballad and jazz styles for rhythm guitar performance
- Fingerstyle — various styles of strums plus arpeggios and plucking patterns using free strokes (tirando)

Melody or Lead
- Pickstyle down-and up-strokes
- Fingerstyle alternating rest strokes (apoyando)

Scales
- G and C major scales in 1st position and 2nd position
- Minor pentatonic scales — Gm pentatonic, Am pentatonic and Em pentatonic

Notation and Theory

Fundamentals
- Staff, bar lines, measures, treble clef, note names, meters, chord frames, tablature, counting music, writing music notation, note values, primary bass, roots, fifths, keys, repeat signs, intervals, sharps, flats, tempo markings, dynamics
- Notes in 1st position
- Notes in 2nd, 3rd and 5th positions for the more advanced students

Theory
- Chords: principal, secondary, embellished, altered
- Common progressions: I-IV-V7, i-iv-V7, ii-V7, I°-vi-ii-V7, i-VII-i, i-VII-VI-V-i

Elements of music
- rhythm, melody, harmony, tone color (timbre) and form

Ear training
- playing by ear

Improvisation

Composition
- learn to write music utilizing the three structural principles: repetition, contrast and variation
- analyze songs performed and studied in class

Vocal Instruction (optional)

- Learn to sing on pitch and discover vocal range and register
- Learn to sing and play an accompaniment on the guitar
- Learn vocal techniques — breath control, tone production, expression, phrasing
- Learn to sing a harmony part

Performance

- Perform songs and notation exercises studied in class
- Perform solo or in small groups for the class
- Present "showcases" or concerts to invited students
- Performance test on achievement standards — chord progression, strums, note playing

Appreciation

- Guest performers/clinicians — invite local studio teachers and performers to the class
- Develop an aesthetic perception for valuing and comparing music
- Develop a historical and cultural awareness of the contribution of music to a society
- Point out the contributions made by various ethnic groups

Major Activities

- Guitar instruction and practice
- Playing accompaniment on the guitar to songs studied in class
- Singing and playing accompaniment on the guitar (optional)
- Performing for the class in small groups or as a soloist
- Listening to a variety of music that represents many styles
- Learning about music fundamentals and theory
- Writing and composing music
- Improvisation
- Viewing music videos
- Individual study and projects

Evaluation

Grades in this class will be determined on the following basis:
- Day to day participation, practice, attitude and effort
- Individual playing and performance tests
- Group performance tests
- Successful completion of various Achievement Standards
- Objective tests on the fundamentals of music
- Maintaining a notebook
- Solo and small group performances before the class
- Working up to your ability — based on the teacher's evaluation of your
    musical aptitude
- This class will observe and follow the school tardy and attendance policy
  as it pertains to grades

UNIT ONE

Chords & Accompaniment

(pages 2–14)

Introduction:
Types of Guitars, Parts of the Guitar
Holding the Guitar
Tuning the Guitar, Names of Strings

Music Fundamentals:
Notes and Rests
Bar lines, Measures and Time Signatures
Staff, Clef Sign, Frames, Tablature

Chords:
C and G7 (3 string chords)
D, A7, G

Accompaniment:
Basic Strum No. 1

Songs:
Marianne, Tom Dooley
He's Got The Whole World
Worried Man Blues
When The Saints Go Marching In
Amazing Grace, Our Land, Surfin'

Learning to Read Music

(pages 62–68)

Introduction:
Playing Techniques
Pickstyle Down-Stroke (∏) and Up-Stroke (V)
Fingerstyle Rest Stroke (*apoyando*)
Note Reading Preparation
Rhythm Drills
Left-hand Drill

Music Fundamentals:
Whole Notes
Half Notes
Quarter Notes
Counting Rhythms
Note Names

Notes:
E, F and G on the 1st String

Songs:
Mist
Chelsie

Supplemental Materials

General Handouts: *Course Description, Student Survey*

Worksheet
- *#1* The Guitar, Parts of the Guitar, Names of Strings
- *#2* Chord Frames, Notes, Bar Lines, 4/4 Time Signature
- *#3* Treble Clef, Note Names, Tablature
- *#4* Writing and Counting Music

Songsheet
- *#1 Rock-a My Soul, Good News, Alouette* (two-chord songs in the key of D)
- *#2 This Train is Bound for Glory, Beautiful Brown Eyes* (three-chord songs in the key of D)

Notesheet
- *#1 First String Warm-Up*

Unit One Test: Covers the material contained in *Worksheets #1–4*

Lesson One

The first day of class can be devoted to getting organized for instruction.
Use or adapt the *Course Description* and *Student Survey* handouts.

Course Description

Sometimes called the "green sheet," the course description usually includes prerequisites, course content, means of evaluation, text and notebook requirements and deadlines for having guitars and materials in class.

Student Survey

In many situations, students are expected to provide their own guitars. While some students will already have a guitar others will need tips on how and where to select a guitar. I suggest giving them the weekend to obtain a guitar. Discuss, display and demonstrate the different types of guitars — nylon string, steel string and electric. I recommend an acoustic guitar but will also allow electric guitars (no amps) in the class.

Selecting a Guitar

The survey will enable you to get familiar with your students' musical backgrounds and knowledge. It identifies the students that will probably move faster in the class and will therefore need to be challenged. The survey will help develop a plan for **differentiating** instruction. You need to know which students can play open or moveable chords on the guitar and which students can already read music. Collect the survey at the end of the period.

Lesson Two

Review dates when all students need to have their notebooks and guitars.
Have students who already have a guitar bring them to class tomorrow. Go over where the guitars will be stored.

Assign textbooks and go over Types Of Guitars (pp. 2 & 3).
Teach the parts of the guitar, names of strings. Pass out *Worksheet #1*.

Audition students

While the students are doing the work sheet, call up students individually who have indicated in the *Student Survey* a knowledge of chords and/or music notation. Have the students who know some chords play for you. Determine and make note of their knowledge of chords, right hand techniques, scales and music notation or tablature. Talk to the students who read music. Their past musical experience, instrumental and vocal, will transfer and will most likely enable them to move faster than the students who are true *beginners*.

Lesson Three

All the students who have guitars should have brought them to class today. This is a good time to assess the condition of each student's instrument and to check for obvious problems such as: moveable bridges out of position; the wrong kind of strings; strings put on incorrectly; "action" that is too high; a warped fingerboard.

Tune and assess guitars

Have each row bring their guitars up to you so you can tune and evaluate them. Have students share with the class where they got their guitars and what they cost. This will help those students still looking for a guitar.

Teach the sitting position and Basic Strum No. 1

Introduce the Sitting Position (p. 4) and teach the Basic Strum No. 1 (p. 9) using the index finger. It is important to have the students rest their forearm on the edge of the guitar just above the bridge bass (p. 8).

Teach C and G7 chords

Explain chord frames, left hand fingering (p. 7), left hand playing position (p. 9), and teach and drill the G7 and C chords (p. 10).

Lesson Four

Check notebooks, tune guitars

All of the students should have an organized binder for the guitar class. The notebook should be organized as set forth in the Course Description and should include all handouts.

Review holding the guitar, Basic Strum No. 1, and the C and G7 chords. Quickly tune the guitars by having students come to you, row by row. Don't be too particular, just get them "in the ball park."

Drill
rest stroke (apoyando)

Introduce the *rest stroke* (p. 63). Play the note reading preparation drills (p. 64) using the rest stroke.

Worksheet #2

Frames, 4/4 time signature, notes, bar lines and staff (pp. 6 and 7) should be introduced as preparation for playing ex. 1, 2, 3 and *Marianne* (p. 10). Have the students complete *Worksheet #2*.

New song
Marianne

Play *Marianne* (p. 10) using the C and G7 chord (3 strings). Play along with the CD or play the melody on the piano. Have the students give a slight emphasis to the first beat of the measure.

Challenge

Some students might be able to play the full C and G7 chord (p. 57).

Lesson Five

Assuming that all of the students now have their guitars, you need to assess and tune these guitars and do a review of all the techniques covered thus far. Circulate around the room and make corrections as needed in regards to holding the guitar, right hand and left hand playing position, playing the C and G7 chords.

Teach listening position

Have the students place their guitars face down on their laps. This is the position to ask for when you plan to speak to the entire class regarding chords, accompaniment, theory, notation, new assignments, etc. It prevents the students from unconsciously playing their guitars at a time you want their full attention.

Introduce pickstyle playing techniques

I suggest that the students learn both pickstyle and fingerstyle techniques. A compromise would be to insist that all students learn fingerstyle techniques and make it optional to learn pickstyle techniques. Introduce pickstyle techniques (p. 8). Review the Basic Strum No. 1 using a pick. It is important that the students hold the pick correctly. Don't allow the middle finger to assist in holding the pick (p.8, fig.3).

Teach and drill the A7 and D chords

Teach the A7 and D chords (p. 11). Stress that the left hand fingernails need to be short and that the fingers need to be placed close but just behind the frets to avoid "buzz." Play ex. 4 and 5 (p. 11). The D chord is more difficult to play because the ring finger is apt to touch the 1st string — *arch the 3rd finger.* Do the following drills:

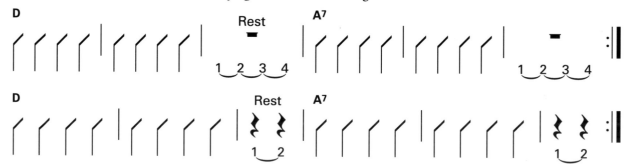

Songsheet #1
two-chord songs

Play ex. 6 and *Tom Dooley* on the CD; *Tracks 3.1* and *3.2*. Repeat and have the class play along. Play *He's Got The Whole World* (p. 12).

Challenge

Some students could use the Bass/Chord Strum (p. 16) on drills, progressions and songs.

Lesson Six

Learning to tune the guitar is one of the more difficult problems facing the beginner. Students need to learn how to match pitch. Demonstrate and go over tuning technique (p. 5). Students need to know how the tuning mechanism works; that is, tightening the strings raises the pitch and loosening the strings lowers the pitch. A good procedure to establish is as follows:

Establish a tuning procedure

- Play the CD, *Track 1* to give tuning pitches to the students as you take roll
- Have students listen to the pitch and attempt to match the pitch using the tuning technique (p. 5)
- Beginning with the 6th string, have the class play the open strings together
- Ask who needs help and have these students bring their guitars up to you or to student helpers

The idea is to develop a tuning procedure that will get the guitars tuned as fast as possible as the students develop their ear for matching pitch. Caution the students that except in rare cases they should not have to move the tuning key more than a half turn or so and that the lower sounding strings generally stay fairly well in tune. Other procedures are to give the students the pitch off of your guitar or from a piano (the different timbre presents a problem for some students). A drop of 3-in-1 oil on the gear teeth will help to keep the tuning mechanism in good shape. The screw inside the gear teeth should not be too tight.

Review the rest stroke, chords and songs

Play rest strokes on the 1st, 2nd and 3rd strings (p. 64), drill the D and A7 chords, review *Tom Dooley* and *He's Got The Whole World.*

Read rhythm drills, practice rest strokes and chords

Play drills 10–14 with the CD, *Track 53* (p. 65). Divide the class in half and have one side of the room play one drill while the other side plays a different drill. Have one side play notes and the other side play chords. For example, have one side play the G7 and the other side plays the 1st fret, 1st string, F or have one side play the A7 chord on a drill and have the other side play the open 1st string, E. There are endless possibilities for using these drills. See some of the other suggestions (p. 65). The benefit is that you are reviewing right hand technique and drilling note values — whole notes, half notes and quarter notes.

Teach the G chord
Worried Man Blues

Introduce the G chord (p. 12), drill it and play ex. 8. Introduce *Worried Man Blues* (p. 13) with the CD, Track 4.

Lesson Seven

Today can be devoted to doing *Worksheet #3* and practice. Before you discuss the worksheet, establish procedures and expectations for practicing. Learning to use their time productively is an important part of this course. Teach them *how to learn.*

Teach the students how to practice

- The quality of the practice is important. Develop good playing habits. Practice with good posture and correct right and left hand playing techniques.
- Frequency and repetition bring results. You are developing muscular and coordination skills that benefit from repetition.
- Develop a *kinesthetic* feeling for the guitar; that is, learn to play strums and chords without looking at your hands.
- Practicing in "real time" is more beneficial then the "stop and start" method. Practice with some sense of a beat.
- Focus on the problem area. Work on small sections at a time.

Complete *Worksheet #3*

Go over *Worksheet #3.* Have students do the worksheet in class, get it checked by you and then put it into their notebooks. Students should then get their guitars out and practice chords, songs and drills covered in class. Circulate around the room to make individual corrections and suggestions.

Lesson Eight

Review

Drill the D, G, A7 chords and review songs.

Teach 3/4 time signature

Introduce and discuss the new 3/4 time signature (p. 13) used in *Amazing Grace.*

Introduce new songs

Play *When The Saints Go Marching In* and *Amazing Grace* (p. 13).

Preparation for reading music
reading readiness drill

Play rhythm drills #15–19 (p. 65) using a variety of playing techniques: rest stokes, down-strokes (pickstyle), chords. The examples on the CD, *Track 54* are all on the open E, 1st string. Left-Hand Drill #20 (p. 65) is an excellent way to form a good left hand playing position.

Challenge
Bass/Chord Strum

Some students could use the Bass/Chord accompaniment on various songs.

Lesson Nine

New song
Mist

Introduce the E and F on the 1st string (p. 66). Play *Mist* (p. 67). The CD is helpful in drilling these exercises as you circulate around the room. Remember that you can remove the melody from the CD by eliminating the right track.

Songsheet #2
three chord songs in D

Songsheet #2 provides additional practice playing the D, G and A7 chords with *This Train* and *Beautiful Brown Eyes.*

Lesson Ten

Review note reading, chords and songs

Drill the E and F on the 1st string (p. 66) and play *Mist* (p. 67). Review and practice chords and songs.

Assignment
achievement standards 1 and 2

All of the students need to play for you individually. Focus their practice on preparation for taking their first chord and notation test. For more details, see Achievement Standards (p.7).

Lesson Eleven

Play new songs
Our Land, Surfin'

Introduce *Our Land* and *Surfin'* (p. 14) to provide more practice on playing the D, G and A7 chords. Have the students play these songs with the CD, *Tracks 6* and *7*.

Practice for test

Provide time for the students to practice for the chord and notation test. Circulate around the room to offer help.

Challenge

Some students could play Basic Strum No. 2 as an accompaniment for *Surfin'*.

Lesson Twelve

Complete *Worksheet #4*

Briefly review the materials included in *Worksheet #4:* Writing and Counting Music.

Review and practice

When the students have completed the worksheet, they should practice for the chord and notation test.

Lessons Thirteen and Fourteen

Evaluation. It generally takes two days to individually test a class of 30 students. Make notes regarding corrections that need to be made in technique, posture, playing position, etc. so that you can follow-up the test with individual teaching. In the interest of time, you can also use group testing. One method is to have all the students play the assignment several times as you grade four or five students. Repeat, as necessary, until you have graded the entire class.

Playing Test
achievement standards 1 and 2

Test the students individually. Grade them from 1–10 on each of the following areas: playing position and technique (right and left hand); ability to play the chords cleanly and without hesitation (speed is not important); ability to read notation by playing *Mist*. Another method of evaluation might be to give a percentage to each part of the overall grade.

Challenge
5th Position

The more advanced students could play the D-G-A7-D chord progression using a more demanding right hand accompaniment. They could play *Mist* in 5th position. Play the E, 2nd string, 5th fret with the first finger and the F, 2nd string, 6th fret with the second finger.

Lesson Fifteen

After presenting the new notation material to the class, meet with students individually or in small groups to go over any part of the chord and notation test that they didn't pass. Teach and make corrections as necessary. Assign a time when students can take a makeup test. The goal is for every student to succeed. Each student must successfully play each of the Achievement Standards. Some students may need more time to pass or perhaps you need to review with them how to practice; maybe they have not been using their time wisely.

New note G, 1st string, 3rd fret	Play ex. 26–30 and *Chelsie* (pp. 67 and 68). Assign *Chelsie* as the next notation test.
Challenge *5th position*	Have the students who already have note reading ability play *Chelsie* in 5th position. Begin with the first finger at the 5th fret, 2nd string. Use the 4th finger to play the G, 2nd string, 8th fret.
Review songs	Play *Surfin'* and *Our Land* with the CD, *Tracks 6* and *7*.
Review test	Discuss, in general, how the the students did on the Achievement Standards Test. Point out what problems were common and what you would like to see improved. Meet with those students who will need to take a makeup on any part of the test. Focus their practice on the problems you observed in the test. Assign a time for the makeup test.

Lesson Sixteen

Review notation, hand out *Notesheet #1*	Review the notes on the 1st string and *Chelsie* (p. 68). For additional practice on playing E, F and G on the 1st string, pass our *Notesheet #1*. Exercise 1 on the *Notesheet* is designed to be played with *Track 52* on the CD (p. 55, ex. 93).
Review for the Unit One Test	Review the material covered in *Worksheets #1–4* to prepare the students for the Unit One Test:

- Parts of the guitar, names of strings, sound of strings
- chord frames, notes, bar lines, 4/4 and 3/4 time signatures
- treble clef, note names, tablature
- writing and counting music

Lessons Seventeen and Eighteen

Playing Test *achievement standard 3*	Test the students individually on their ability to play *Chelsie* (p, 68)
Students organize notebooks	As you are testing, the other students should be practicing and reviewing for the Unit One Test. They could also be getting their notebooks organized so that they can turn them in to you on Unit One Test day.

Lesson Nineteen

Collect notebooks, **Give Unit Test**	Give the Unit One Test and collect the student notebooks.

UNIT TWO

Chords & Accompaniment

(pages 15–23)

Music Fundamentals & Theory:
Eighth Notes, Slashes, Mute Sign
Tablature
Tonality, Principal Chords I, IV, V
Key of D, Key of G
Playing by Ear
Primary Bass or Root of the D, G and A7
Backbeat
Swing Eighths, Shuffle

Chords:
Review D, G, A7
A, C, D7

Accompaniment:
Basic Strum No. 2
Free Stroke (thumb)
Bass/Chord Strum
Mute Technique
Latin Strum
Rock/Mute Strum
Chord/Mute Strum
Blues Strum

Songs and Progressions:
Bye, Love
Basic Rock/Blues Progression (in D)
Ex, 13, Ex. 19
Basic Rock/Blues Progression (in G)
Ex. 21, *Just A Closer Walk With Thee*

Learning to Read Music

(pages 69–73)

Music Fundamentals:
Tempo Markings
Quarter Rest
Repeat Sign
Dotted Half Note
3/4 Time Signature
Dal Segno (*D. S. al Fine*)
Tie

Notes:
B, C, D on the 2nd String
Review the Notes on the 1st and 2nd Strings

Songs:
B-C Mix. Easy Rock
Breezin', Rock Out
Prelude, Sort of Blue
Mary Ann

Supplemental Materials

Worksheet
- #5 Eighth Notes, Primary Bass, Keys, Quarter Rest
- #6 Tempo Markings, Repeat Signs, Dotted Half Notes, Tie, Counting

Songsheet
- #3 *Gotta Travel On, La Cucaracha* (Key of G)

Notesheet
- # 1 *Blues/Rock Riff, First Duet, Easy Does It*

Tabsheet
- #1 Exercises 1, 2 and 3

Improvisation Sheet
- #1 Gm Pentatonic Scale, *Gm Pentatonic Solo*

Unit Two Test: Covers the material contained in *Worksheets #5–6*

Lesson One

Eighth notes

Introduce eighth notes (p. 15). Have the students play various eighth note rhythms on chords and open strings. Use rote exercises and rhythm patterns you could write on the board. Play Basic Strum No. 2 (p. 15, ex. 9).

Bass/Chord strum

Present and explain primary bass notes. Drill the Bass/Chord strum, ex. 10 (p. 16). Assignment is to memorize the roots for the D, G and A7 chords.

Play *Bye, Love* with the CD, *Track 9* (p. 16).

B and C on the 2nd string

Introduce the notes on the 2nd string (p. 69) and play ex. 31, 32, 33 and *B-C Mix.*

Challenge
4th and 5th position

Have more advanced students play the B and C on the 3rd string, 4th and 5th fret when they play *B-C Mix.*

Lesson Two

Review

Review eighth notes, the Basic Strum No. 2 and notes on the 2nd string.

Play the D-G-A7-D chord progression using a Bass/Chord strum. Play the root of the chord on the first beat and strum on beats 2, 3, 4. The roots of these chords need to be memorized.

Review songs

Play *Surfin'* and *Our Land* (p. 14) using the Basic Strum No. 2. Review *Bye, Love* (p. 16).

Lesson Three

New note, D on the 2nd string
Easy Rock

Introduce the D on the 2nd string (p. 70). Play ex. 34, 35, 36, 37 and then review the notes on the 1st and 2nd strings. Play and then assign *Easy Rock*, notation achievement standard 4, for future testing.

A chord

Teach the A chord (p.17). Play the *Basic Blues/Rock Progression* (p.17) with *Track 10.* Play ex. 12 and 13.

Challenge
4th and 5th position

More advanced students could learn to play *Easy Rock* in higher positions. Have them begin in 4th position, 1st finger on the 3rd string, 4th fret. Shift into 5th position at measure 3. In measure 7, play the C on the 3rd string, 5th fret and then shift the 1st finger down to the 4th fret (4th position) to play the B.

Lesson Four

Worksheet #5

Discuss the music fundamentals contained in *Worksheet # 5:* Eighth Notes, Primary Bass, Keys, Quarter Rest. Have the students do this assignment in class.

Practice

When students complete the worksheet, they should hand it in and practice for the next test assignment, *Easy Rock* (p. 70). They could also review chords and primary bass notes.

Lesson Five

Review

Review the *Basic Rock/Blues Progression* (p. 17) with CD *Track 10*. Play ex. 13 with *Track 11*.

Review *Easy Rock* (p. 70). Play *Breezin'* and *Rock Out* (p. 71). Go over Tempo Markings, the Quarter Rest and the Repeat Sign.

Mute Technique

Introduce the Mute Technique, the Latin Strum and the Rock/Mute Strum (pp. 18 and 19). Drill ex. 18 and 19 with the CD.

Lesson Six

Fingerstyle Hand Position
free stroke readiness drills

Tabsheet #1

As preparation for developing right hand fingerstyle techniques, introduce the Basic Fingerstyle Hand Position (p. 86). Pass out *Tabsheet #1* and drill ex. 1, 2 and 3. It is very important for the students to *plant* the hand in position before they play the exercises. Circulate around the room to correct and make adjustments in the arm and hand position.

- the forearm should be resting on the edge of the guitar
- the wrist should be straight
- the fingers should be placed over the rosette
- the thumb should be rigid, straight and extend beyond the fingers toward the sound hole

Practice
achievement standards 4 and 5

In preparation for the test, practice *Easy Rock* and the G-C-D-G chord progression using the Bass/Chord Strum.

Lessons Seven and Eight

Notesheet #1 — additional
three string songs

To provide more drill and practice playing the notes on the 1st and 2nd strings, take out *Notesheet #1* and play through *Blues/Rock Riff* and First *Duet* with the suggested CD *Tracks*. Review *Easy Rock*

Playing Test
achievement standards 4 and 5

While students practice the new songs, chords and *Tabsheet* exercises, begin to test them individually on the achievement standards 4 and 5.

Lesson Nine

Tonality

Attempt to play several two and three chord songs "by ear" to develop the concept of tonality and a sense of how the I, IV and V7 chords function in music (p.20).

Key of G, C chord

Introduce the Key of G and the C chord (p. 21).

Basic Rock/Blues Progression
Key of G

Play the *Basic Rock/Blues Progression* (p. 21) with *Track 15* of the CD. Play it using a variety of strums: Basic Strum No. 2, Bass/Chord Strum, Latin Strum, Rock/Mute Strum.

Challenge
moveable chords

Students who already know these open string chords could begin learning the moveable G, C and D7 (p. 61). The C chord requires a third finger bar technique (p. 60).

Lesson Ten

Review

From *Tabsheet #1*, play ex. 1, 2 and 3. Review the Mute Technique (p.18). Play *Breezin'* and *Rock Out* (p. 71).

Swing Eighths, Blues Strum

Introduce Swing Eighths (p. 22) and the shuffle rhythm to the students. Do various rote and written rhythm drills to teach this rhythm. Demonstrate how the Rock/Mute Strum becomes the Blues Strum when you play *swing 8ths*.

Challenge

Some students may be able to play *Rock Out* in 5th position.

Lesson Eleven

Teach and Assign
Prelude

Introduce the Dotted Half Note, 3/4 Time and Dal Segno (p. 72) and then present and assign *Prelude* which is achievement standard 6. Play this solo with the CD, *Track 64*. There may be some students who will be able to play the accompaniment or a simplified version of it (chords and arpeggios).

Worksheet #6

Pass out and go over the material covered in *Worksheet # 6*: Tempo Markings, Repeat Signs, Dotted Half Notes, Counting. Have the students do this assignment in class.

Lesson Twelve

Teach the D7 Chord

Strumming 8 beats on each chord, and then 4 beats, teach the D7 chord by drilling the following chord progressions:

- D7-G-D7 The 3rd finger acts as a *guide*. Keep the 3rd finger in contact with the 1st string as you move between these chords.
- C-D7 Do not lift the 1st finger of the left hand when moving from the C to the D7. The 1st finger is *common* to both chords and can lead you from the C to the D7 chord.

Review
Prelude

Play *Prelude*. Make certain that the students that are using rest strokes are alternating between *i* and *m*. For pickstyle players, check to see that the pick is held correctly. The middle finger should not be used in holding the pick.

Improvisation Sheet #1
G Minor Pentatonic Solo

Pass out and explain how the Minor Pentatonic can be used to improvise a solo over the blues progression. Have one student strum a G chord as you play short phrases. Have the students play back (echo) the phrases. Limit the amount of notes and use a lot of repetition.

Limiting yourself to C, Bb, D and G, play short riffs over the C or C7 chord. Have the students echo. Using only D, C and F, play riffs on the D7 chord. It would be a good idea to start and end on the root of each chord. Demonstrate this on the piano or any other instrument if you are not comfortable on the guitar.

Review how to read tablature and demonstrate the scale and the *G Minor Pentatonic Solo*.

Lesson Thirteen

Check the Mute and Blues Strum Technique

Do the mute technique again and check the student's ability to play the Blues Strum.

Drill Chord Progression
achievement standard 7

Drill the following chord progression using 8 and then 4 beats per measure: D-G-A7-D-G-C-D7-G. Reiterate the importance of memorizing the root of every chord. Play the progression using the Bass/Chord Strum. Review the *transportation* between chords, that is, the use of GUIDE and COMMON fingers when moving from one chord to another. Assign this chord progression for future testing: achievement standard 7.

Teach a new song
Just A Closer Walk With Thee

Play the Blues Strum with the CD, ex. 25, *Track 18*. Introduce *Just A Closer Walk With Thee* (p. 23) with the CD, *Track 19*.

Review Minor Pentatonic

Review the G Minor Pentatonic scale and solo. Have the students play the chord changes while you or a student plays the written solo. Encourage the students to work in groups of two — one person playing the solo as the other plays the chords.

Challenge

Encourage students to improvise their own solo.

Lesson Fourteen

Play *Tabsheet #1* exercises and practice for playing tests

Begin by drilling the fingerstyle patterns presented in the *Tabsheet #1* handout. Review ex. 1–3 and then try playing the rest of them. Review and practice for a playing test on *Prelude* and the chord progression D-G-A7-D-G-C-D7-G. These are achievement standards 6 and 7.

Songsheet #3

For additional practice in playing in the Key of G, pass out and play the songs in *Songsheet #3*. Suggest some accompaniment patterns.

Lessons Fifteen and Sixteen

Playing Test
achievement standard 6

Test the students individually on their ability to play *Prelude*.

While they are waiting to be tested, students should practice chords, songs, improvisation and work on the organization of their notebooks which will be collected for a grade at the end of this unit.

Lesson Seventeen

Drill chords, Tab and songs

Drill the chords. Play the *Tabsheet #1* exercises. Play some songs.

Complete *Notesheet #1*

Review and play the songs from *Notesheet #1*. Introduce and demonstrate *Easy Does It*. Use the CD to accompany these songs or divide the class up and have half play melody and half play the chords. Create a bass part by having some students play the roots of the chords.

Encourage improvisation

Review and work with students on developing a solo based on the G Minor Pentatonic scale. Seek volunteers who might be willing to play for the class.

Lesson Eighteen

This could be a practice day in preparation for the chord test, achievement standard 7. Impress on the students the importance of developing a good technique. Review the playing positions and how you will be grading. Suggest that they check the clarity of their chords by playing one string at a time. Chord forms and roots must be memorized.

Lesson Nineteen

Notation songs
Sort of Blue, Mary Ann

Introduce the Tie (p. 73) and the two new note reading songs *Sort of Blue* and *Mary Ann*. Use the CD, *Track 65* to help present *Sort of Blue*. Divide the class in half and have one side play the melody for *Mary Ann* while the other half plays the chords. Add a bass part on the roots and a harmony part from notes in the chords.

Lesson Twenty

Review

Review *Sort of Blue* and *Mary Ann*.

Other tuning methods

If you haven't done this already, discuss tuning methods with the students. Explain and demonstrate how to tune the guitar to the piano. Every student needs to be able to locate the correct keys on the piano. Discuss and demonstrate how to tune the guitar to itself (p. 5). Go through the steps described in fig. 1–5.

Review playing test

Review the playing test: achievement standard 7.

Lessons Twenty-One and Twenty-Two

Playing Test
achievement standard 7

Test the students individually on the chord progression. Technique, posture and playing position is an important part of the grade.

Lesson Twenty-Three

In preparation for the test, review the music fundamentals covered in both Units One and Two. Have a few students come to the board to practice writing the counting under rhythm exercises and the names under the notes. Pass out music paper and have all the students practice writing music. Review how you want their notebooks to be organize and allow them some time to work on them.

Lesson Twenty-Four

Unit Test

Administer the Unit Two Test and collect the notebooks.

UNIT THREE

Chords & Accompaniment

(pages 24–32)

Music Fundamentals & Theory:
Repeat Signs, First and Second Endings
Primary Bass (root)
vi (Em) and ii (Am) chord in the Key of G
Tie, ii (Em) chord in the Key of D
I-vi-IV-V Chord Progression
I-vi-ii-V Chord Progression
ii-V-I Chord Progression
Key of A, Principal Chords

Chords:
Em, Dsus, Am, E and E7
A7 (optional fingering)
Challenge Chords: A, A7, D7, E7
Power Chords: A5, C5, D5, E5
Moveable Power Chords

Accompaniment:
Double Bass/Chord Strum
Syncopated Strum
Blues Strum (review)
Blues Shuffle
Right Hand Mute

Songs and Progressions:
Ex. 28, Ex. 29, *Dig It*, Ex. 31
Ex. 34, Ex. 37, *Help*
Ex. 40 *(Basic Rock/Blues in A)*
Ex. 41, Ex. 42 *(8 Bar Blues)*
Ex. 44 *(Blues Shuffle in A)*, Ex. 46

Learning to Read Music

(pages 74–78)

Music Fundamentals:
First and Second Endings
Da Capo *(D.C. al Fine)*
Half Step, Whole Step
Sharps and Flats
Major Scale
G Major Scale
Key Signature
Key of G, Principal Chords

Notes:
G and A on the 3rd String
Review of the Notes on the 1st, 2nd and 3rd Strings
F# on the 1st String

Songs:
*Jingle Bells, Peaceful Feeling
G Scale Study, Folk Song*

Supplemental Materials

Worksheet
- #7 Repeat Signs
- #8 Note Names, Chord Names, Roots, Principal Chords, Blues
- #9 Half and Whole Steps, Major Scales, Music Symbols

Songsheet
- #4 *Frankie and Johnny, Cielito Lindo* (Key of A)

Notesheet
- #2 *Three String Warm-Up, Movin', Friends, Jasmine Flower*

Tabsheet
- #1 Exercises 4, 5, 6, 7, 8, 9 and 10

Improvisation Sheet
- #2 A Minor Pentatonic Scale, *A Minor Pentatonic Solo*

Unit Three Test: Covers the material contained in *Worksheets #7–9*

Lesson One

Continue to use the Rhythm Drills (p. 65) to develop reading skills. Play chords, notes, create ensembles, divide the class and combine two or more drills. Have some students play a chord while others play rest strokes on the notes in the chord.

Em chord	Introduce the Em chord normal and optional fingerings (p. 24). Some students find the optional fingering easier since it has a *common* finger with the G (first finger, 2nd fret, 5th string) and C chord (second finger, 2nd fret, 4th string); also, the movement to the A7 chord is facilitated by the fact that the fingers remain on the 2nd fret. Students should memorize the root (R) of the chord. Drill ex. 27.
Chord progression	Play ex. 28 with the CD, *Track 20.* First play the exercise with the Basic Strum No. 1 or No. 2 and then try playing it with the Bass/Chord Strum notated in the exercise.
Tabsheet #1	Review ex. 1–3, and drill ex. 4–8.

Lesson Two

Double Bass/Chord Strum *achievement standard 8*	Review ex. 28 and then present the Double Bass/Chord Strum (p. 25). Drill this strum on various chords and then play ex. 29. This is a very common chord progression (I-vi-IV-V7). Students should learn the numerical way of referring to chords. Play along with the CD, *Track 21.* Assign this exercise and Double Bass/Chord Strum for future testing — achievement standard 8.
G and A on the 3rd string	Drill new notes G and A on the 3rd string (p. 74). Play ex. 40–43 and review all of the notes on the *treble* strings in ex. 44.

Lesson Three

Chord review and drill	Start with a chord review. A good way to drill chords is to start the progression and while the students are playing, announce the next chord destination ("going to the G chord"), and then *count* 1–2 ready *change* (make the chord change on the 5th beat). Try drilling the following using the Double Bass/Chord Strum: D-G-A7-D-G-Em-C-D7-G.
Notesheet #2 *Three String Warm-Up*	Play the *Three String Warm-Up.* Divide the class and have half play the notes and the others play chord accompaniment. Try different strums. Add a bass part by having some students play the roots of the chords using the following rhythm:

Lesson Four

Worksheet #7	Go over the material contained in the *Worksheet #7:* Repeat Signs. Pass out the assignment. When they are done, they should hand it in and practice for the rest of the period.
Improvisation *challenge*	During the time the students are doing the worksheet, you could hear and give credit to any students who may have developed a solo using the G Minor Pentatonic scale. Arrange to have students who are willing perform for the class: advanced achievement standard 1.

Lesson Five

Dsus chord	Drill the Dsus chord (p. 25): Dsus-D-Dsus-G.
New song *Dig It*	Explain the first and second ending and then play *Dig It* with the CD, *Track 22.* Use a Double Bass/Chord Strum.
Notesheet #2 *Movin'*	Review the notes on the treble strings and then play *Three String Warm-Up.* Introduce and practice *Movin'* on *Notesheet #2.* This song can also be played with *Track 22* or you can have the students play the chords. Make up a bass part. Try adding a harmony part.

Lesson Six

Review	Review *Dig It* and *Movin'.*
Syncopated Strum	Teach the Syncopated Strum (p. 26). Go over the explanation in the book. It is important to play this strum with the proper accent. Students who have difficulty with the strum usually succeed when they play it with successive down-strokes.
Ex. 31	Play ex. 31 with the CD, *Track 23* using the Syncopated Strum.
New song *Peaceful Feeling*	Go over *D. C. al Fine* (p. 75) and play *Peaceful Feeling.* Review the Tie in measures 7 and 8. Assign this song for future testing — achievement standard 9.

Lesson Seven

Am Chord	Introduce the Am chord (p. 26) as the ii chord in the Key of G and its tendency to resolve to the D7 (V7) chord. Drill ex. 33 pointing out the *common* finger that allows for smooth transportation between the two chords.
Drills	Play ex. 34 and 35. Either fingering of the Em will work. The normal fingering (second and third fingers) shares a similar shape and position (2nd fret) with the Am chord; the normal fingering has a common finger with the G chord.
Ex. 36	Play ex. 36 with the CD, *Track 25* using the Syncopated Strum.
Review	Review the notation assignment. Play *Peaceful Feeling* (p. 75).

Lesson Eight

Review	Drill the chord progression ex. 29 (p. 25) using the Double Bass/Chord Strum. Play ex. 33–36. Play various exercises on *Tabsheet #1.*
Notesheet #2	Review *Movin'* and introduce *Friends* on *Notesheet #2.* Use the CD to accompany these songs, *Tracks 22* and *43.* Review the use of the Tie in measures 7 and 8.
Challenge	Some students may be able to play the chord changes to *Friends.*

Lesson Nine

Em chord	Discuss the Em chord and its function as the ii chord in the Key of D.
Chord drills *Help*	Play ex. 37 with the CD, *Track 26* and ex. 38. Play *Help* with the CD, *Track 27*.
Practice	Practice for the playing test.

Lessons Ten and Eleven

Playing Test *achievement standards 8 and 9*	Test the students individually on their ability to play ex. 29 and *Peaceful Feeling*.

While they are waiting to be tested, students should practice and review various chord and notation assignments. This is also a good time for students to investigate **supplemental song books** you may have available in the classroom.

If you have **practice rooms**, develop some guidelines, rules and regulations on how students are to use them You might allow some students to work together in the practice rooms during this individual testing time. This depends on your facilities and your ability to observe the rooms as you test students.

Lesson Twelve

E and E7 chords	Discuss the Principal Chords in the Key of A and introduce the E and E7 chords. Have students memorize the root of the chord.
Transportation *new A chord fingering*	All fingerings of the A chord have advantages and disadvantages. In addition to the fingerings for the A chord presented earlier (p. 17), the following shape will appeal to some beginners, fig. 1, because it shares a *common* finger with the D chord and contains a *guide* finger to the E7 chord. Drill the A-D-E7-A chord progression.  fig. 1
Play ex. 40	Play ex. 40 with the CD, *Track 28* using a Blues Strum or shuffle rhythm.
Challenge	Play moveable versions of the Principal Chords in A. Review the moveable G, C and D7 chords (p. 61). Move each chord up to the 5th fret and you will have A, D and E7.

Lesson Thirteen

Review	Drill the chords in the Key of A and play and review ex. 40. Drill all of the exercises on *Tabsheet #1*. Play these patterns on various chords. The thumb plucks the root of the chord. The finger pattern remains the same.
Songsheet #4 *Frankie and Johnny*	For more practice playing in the Key of A, pass out *Songsheet # 4* and play *Frankie and Johnny*.
Intervals, Sharps	Introduce the Half Step, Whole Step, Sharp and F# (p.76). Play ex. 45.
Major Scale *achievement standard 10*	Explain the structure of the Major Scale, that is, the arrangement of whole steps and half steps and where they occur. Introduce the G scale on the guitar. Play the *G Scale Study* (p. 77) with the CD, *Track 67*. Assign this study for future testing—achievement standard 10.

Lesson Fourteen

Review	Review ex. 40, *Frankie and Johnny*, and the *G Scale Study*.
Play ex. 41	Play ex. 41 with the CD, *Track 29*.
Improvisation Sheet #2 *A Minor Pentatonic*	Present and discuss the A Minor Pentatonic Scale described and diagramed on the *Improvisation Sheet #2*. Practice ex. 2. Point out the importance of knowing where the roots of the chords occur in the scale. It is one these roots that the beginning riffs should begin and end. Target these notes. Demonstrate the *A Minor Pentatonic Solo* pointing out how the roots are targeted and that the short riffs are repeated. This solo can be played with *Track 28* or *Track 31*.
Challenge	Use the scale to create your own original solo. Use the first position scale or the moveable pattern which occurs at the 5th fret.

Lesson Fifteen

Review the A Minor Pentatonic Scale and *A Minor Pentatonic Solo*. Continue to encourage improvisation. Play some short *call-and-response* riffs; that is, you play and the students answer. Use any instrument.

New song *8-Bar Blues*	Introduce the *8-Bar Blues*, ex. 42, with *Track 30* (p. 30). Encourage students to try the alternate chord forms presented in the challenge section. The A and A7 are simplified versions. Assign the *8-Bar Blues* played with a Blues Strum for future testing: achievement standard 11.
Notesheet #2 *Jasmine Flower*	For additional practice reading and playing notes on the treble strings play *Jasmine Flower*. Create an ensemble by having some students play an accompaniment and others a bass part.
Challenge	Some students could create a fingerstyle accompaniment using one of the patterns from *Tabsheet #1*.

Lesson Sixteen

Worksheet #8 *practice*	Lecture the material covered in *Worksheet #8:* Note Names, Chord Names, Roots, Principal Chords, Blues. Have the students do the assignment in class. When they have finished, they should turn it in to be checked or you could go over the worksheet when they bring it up to you. I don't grade worksheets but insist that they be done correctly. After checking them, they should be returned to the students so they can use them to study for the Unit Test. Students should use the rest of the period for practice.

Lesson Seventeen

Review songs *improvisation*	Play the *8-Bar Blues*, *G Scale Study*. Play *Track 28* and the *A Minor Pentatonic Solo*. See if there are any volunteers who would like to play a solo on this chord progression.
New song *Blues Shuffle in A*	While the *Blues Shuffle in A* (p. 31) can be played fingerstyle (with the thumb or index finger), it can be more effectively played pickstyle (using successive down-strokes). To demonstrate ex. 44, play *Track 31*. Demonstrate the variation, ex. 45.
Challenge	Develop a solo using the A minor pentatonic scale.

Lesson Eighteen

New notation song
Folk Song

Demonstrate the *Folk Song* (p. 78) with the CD, *Track 68*. Point out that the song is based on a descending G major scale. Play the chord accompaniment and create a bass part. Some students may be able to play the written accompaniment.

Practice

Practice for a playing test: achievement standards 10 and 11.

Lessons Nineteen and Twenty

Playing Test
achievement standards 10 and 11

Have each student play for you individually. Until they are tested, they need to be practicing, working out of supplemental song books, in practice rooms, rehearsing together.

Lesson Twenty-One

Review

Review the *Blues Shuffle in A* (p. 31). The written *A Minor Pentatonic* goes well with this accompaniment pattern. Some students might work on combining the two into a duet. You can always add a bass part.

Power chords

Introduce the Power Chords (p. 32) with *Track 32*. Many of the students will already know these chords, including the moveable forms. They can assist in teaching the rest of the students and demonstrating for the class.

Challenge

Create a solo based on the A minor pentatonic scale for the power chords, ex. 46.

Lesson Twenty-Two

Worksheet #9

Go over *Worksheet #9:* Half and Whole Step, Major Scales, Music Symbols. Have the students complete this assignment in class and then spend the rest of the period practicing.

Optional testing

This could be an opportunity to test students who might be ready to pass the advanced achievement standard 2 and for you to follow-up on the Playing Test (achievement standards 10 and 11) with students that need some help, correction or a retest.

Lesson Twenty-Three

Review

Play various songs and chord progressions.

Notebook preparation

Allow students some time to organize their notebooks according to the *Course Description* outline.

Lesson Twenty-Four

Review
Unit Test

Review for the Unit Three Test. Lecture on all of the material that will be included. Do some practice at the board with some students. Work with students who need extra help.

Lesson Twenty-Five

Unit Test

Administer Unit Three Test and collect the notebooks.

UNIT FOUR

Chords & Accompaniment

(pages 33–40)

Music Fundamentals & Theory:
Key of E, Principal Chords
Turnaround
Sixteenth Notes
Minor Keys
Key of Em, Principal Chords
III-VI-VII Chords in Minor Keys
Chord Embellishments

Chords:
A7 (optional fingering)
C7, Am7, Gmaj7, Cmaj7
F#m7b5 (challenge chord)

Accompaniment:
Blues Techniques — Slide and Lift
Rock Ballad Strum and Variation
Latin Strum Variation

Songs and Progressions:
Ex. 49. (*12-Bar Blues*)
Ex. 52 (*Blues Shuffle in E*)
Ex. 54 (*Blues Shuffle*), Ex. 58 (*Rock Ballad Strum*)
Ex. 60 (*Minor Blues*), Ex. 61 (*Walking The Bass*)
Ex. 64 (*Jazz*), Ex. 65 (*Latin*)

Learning to Read Music

(pages 79–83)

Music Fundamentals:
Natural Sign
Leger Lines
Eighth Notes

Playing Technique:
Shifting
Pickstyle Up-stroke (∨)

Notes:
G# and A on the 1st String
Open Bass Strings — D, A, E

Songs:
Spanish Song
Harvest
Celebrate
Ode To Joy

Supplemental Materials

Worksheet
• *#10* Principal Chords, Embellishments, Symbols, Sixteenth Notes, Analysis

Songsheet
• *#5* C. C. Rider, John B. Sails, Swing Low
• *#6* Hava Nagila, When Johnny Comes Marching Home

Notesheet
• *#3* Round, G Boogie, Am Etude, Love Her

Tabsheet
• *#2* Exercises 11, 12 and 13

Improvisation Sheet
• *#3* Em Pentatonic Scale, *Em Pentatonic Solo*

Unit Four Test: Covers the material contained in *Worksheet #6–10*

Lesson One

Introduce and drill the Principal Chords in the Key of E: E, A and B7. The transportation between the E and B7 chord is made more smoothly when using the 2nd finger as a *guide* finger, ex. 48. Any of the various A chord fingerings are workable. The optional fingering for the A7 is the most logical since it keeps the fingers on the 2nd fret of the guitar. Practice the following chord progression: E-A-B7-E. Play the progression using various strums.

B7 chord	The *12-Bar Blues*, ex 49 (p. 33), has a turnaround in the first ending. The V7 chord is most often used to send you back to the beginning of the song.
New song *12-Bar Blues*	Play the CD, *Track 33*. The strum used on the recording is the Double Bass/Chord Strum.
Assignment *achievement standard 12*	For future testing, practice E-A-B7-E-Em-Am-B7-Em: achievement standard 12. Point out that the E, Em (normal fingering) and B7 share a *common* finger, Am and B7 share a *common* finger and the 2nd and 3rd fingers are on the same frets in the Em and Am.

Lesson Two

Blues techniques *slide and lift*	Introduce and demonstrate the Slide and Lift (p.34), ex. 50 and 51, *Tracks 34* and *35*. The tablature and the chord frame above the tablature help to clarify these techniques. In the beginning, omit the mute from the exercises.
Review and new song *C.C. Rider*	Review the *12-Bar Blues* using various strums. Try adding the *lift* and *slide* techniques. Handout *Songsheet #5* and play *C. C. Rider*.
New notes and fundamentals *G# and A, 1st string*	Introduce the Natural Sign, Leger Lines and G# and A on the 1st string. Play ex. 47, 48 and 49.

Lesson Three

New song *Spanish Song*	Review ex. 47, 48 and 49 (p. 79). Discuss Shifting and play ex. 50 (p. 80). Play the *Spanish Song* with the CD, *Track 69*. Remember the melody can be eliminated in the recording by taking out the right channel.
Create an accompaniment	Some students will be able to create a plucking arpeggio pattern for an accompaniment. Students who are working ahead in the book could learn the written accompaniment.
Review	Play the *12-Bar Blues*, ex. 49 (p. 33).
Improvisation Sheet #3 *E Minor Pentatonic*	The *E Minor Pentatonic Scale* can be used to create a solo for the E blues progression. Learn the fingering in first position and become aware of the location of the roots of the chords. Each phrase or riff in the *E Minor Pentatonic Solo* ends on the root of the chord. Students should learn the solo and then attempt to create their own. More advanced students can experiment with the *moveable* version of this scale. Use *Track 36* or another guitarist to play the accompaniment.

Lesson Four

Review
Spanish Song

Review shifting ex. 50 and *Spanish Song* (p. 80). Assign for future testing: achievement standard 13.

Bass strings D, A, E
Round

Introduce the Open Bass Strings (p. 81) and play ex. 51–53. For addition music reading, play *Round* from *Notesheet #3*. It contains the D, open 4th string.

Improvisation

Work with students individually on developing a solo on the E minor pentatonic scale.

Lesson Five

It is important that you keep the *Tabsheet* exercises going. If the students can play the patterns on the open strings, have them play the patterns on various chords as is notated in *Tabsheet #1*. All of this preparation and *readiness* drilling will make the fingerstyle techniques presented in the next unit go very smoothly.

Tabsheet #1 and 2
fingerstyle free strokes (tirando)

Play the various patterns presented on *Tabsheet #1* on the E, A and B7 chords. Play ex. 11 on *Tabsheet #2*.

New song
Blues Shuffle in E

Introduce the *Blues Shuffle in E* (p. 35) with the CD, *Track 36*. It is best to play this blues lick with a pick.

Challenge

Instead of playing what is written for measure 9 in ex. 52, substitute the measure notated in ex. 53.

Lesson Six

Review

Review the *Blues Shuffle in E* and *C.C. Rider*. Make sure that the students are playing swing eighths.

New notation songs
Harvest, G Boogie

Review and play the *Spanish Song*, Open Bass String ex. 51–53 and then introduce *Harvest* (p. 81). Divide the students between the *solo* and the *accompaniment*. Some students could add a fingerstyle arpeggio accompaniment on the chords. For additional practice, review *Round* and play the *G Boogie* on *Notesheet #3*.

E6, A6, A7 chords

Introduce the new chord embellishments (p. 36).

New song
Blues Shuffle

Play the *Blues Shuffle*, ex. 54 on the CD, *Track 37*. Play swing eighths.

Lesson Seven

Review and practice for the Playing Test

Review and practice for the playing test: achievement standards 12 and 13. Drill the chord progression: E-A-B7-E-Em-Am-B7-Em using any strum. The emphasis is on the clarity of the chords and moving from one to the other without hesitation. Tempo is not important.

Spanish Song should display good right hand fingerstyle technique: alternating rest stokes with the index and middle fingers.

Circulate around the room to give students tips on what they need to correct in order to receive a good grade on this playing test.

Lessons Eight and Nine

Performance Days
develop and schedule

When not being tested, students could pursue, develop and rehearse individual and group performance projects. Now that the students are advancing, it is motivational to plan for performance days. Depending on the class, these performance days could occur every two or three weeks. Many interesting things develop when you give the students a little direction in the curriculum.

Playing Test
achievement standards 12 and 13

Test each student individually on achievement standard 12 and 13. Also test any student who may be ready for advance achievement standard 3.

Lesson Ten

Sixteenth notes

Introduce Sixteenth Notes (p. 37). Practice tapping and counting rhythms. Have students tap quarter notes, eighth notes and then sixteenth notes. Use fig. 2 and 3 to assist in developing the concept of playing notes on the down and up part of the beat. Play ex. 55, 56 and 57 slowly paying particular attention to the pick direction (⊓ V).

New songs
Rock Ballad, John B. Sails
Swing Low

Play *Rock Ballad Strum*, ex. 58 with the CD, *Track 38* (p. 37). Stress or give emphasis to the first beat of each measure. For additional practice playing the chords in E, play *John B. Sails* and *Swing Low* from *Songsheet #5*

Tabsheet #2

Review *Tabsheet #2*, ex. 11 and introduce ex. 12. Check for good right hand position.

Lesson Eleven

Worksheet #10

Review the music fundamentals contained in *Worksheet # 10*: Principal Chords, Embellishments, Symbols, Sixteenth Notes, Analysis. Students should complete the worksheet in class so that you can check it for accuracy.

Performance day

When students have completed the worksheet, they can practice for the first performance day presentation.

Lesson Twelve

Minor Keys
Key of Em

Introduce Minor Keys and the Principal Chords in the Key of Em (p. 38): Em, Am and B7 (i, iv, V7). In this book, a lower case Roman numeral indicates a minor chord. The i and iv chords are always minor chords in a minor Key. As mentioned earlier, the transportation between the chords will be easier if students notice *common* fingers and fingers that are in the same relative position (same frets) on the fingerboard.

C7 chord

Practice the C7 chord moving to the B7 chord.

New song
12-Bar Minor Blues

Play the *12-Bar Minor Blues,* p. 38, ex. 60 with the CD, *Track 39.* Try playing the progression with the Rock/Mute Strum (p. 19).

Challenge

Create a solo using the E minor pentatonic scale.

Review

Review the *Rock Ballad Strum,* ex. 58 (p. 37).

Lesson Thirteen

Review

Review the *12-Bar Minor Blues.*

Eighth Notes

Review Eighth Notes and pickstyle and fingerstyle playing techniques (p.82). With the CD, drill ex. 54–57, *Track 71.* Repeat the exercises on various notes and strings.

New notation song
Celebrate

Introduce *Celebrate* with the CD, *Track 72* (p. 83). Divide the class between the *solo* and *chord* accompaniment. Some students could play moveable chord forms. Create a bass part. Assign this song for future testing: achievement standard 14.

Challenge
D Minor Pentatonic

The melody to *Celebrate* is based on the D minor pentatonic scale. Learn the scale and create an original solo on this chord progression. Practice with the CD or another guitarist.

Fingering 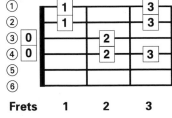   *Note Names*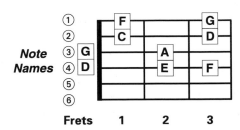

Lesson Fourteen

Review

Review *Celebrate* and the *12-Bar Minor Blues.* Continue to encourage and help students develop improvised solos using the minor pentatonic scale.

Tabsheet #2

Review ex. 11 and 12. Introduce ex. 13.

New song
Hava Nagila

For additional practice in the Key of Em, play *Hava Nagila* from *Songsheet #6.* Use a Bass/Chord Strum or develop an accompaniment based on ex. 13 from *Tabsheet #2.*

Lesson Fifteen

Review

Play *Hava Nagila* and other chord songs.

New song and progressions
Walking the Bass

Introduce ex. 61, *Walking the Bass* (p. 39), with the CD, *Track 40.* Assign this exercise for future testing: achievement standard 15.

Play ex. 62 and 63. Drill the chords and try different accompaniment patterns. Some students could play the arpeggio pattern notated for this song on page 48.

New notation song
Am Etude

Review *Round* and *G Boogie* from *Notesheet #3.* Introduce the *Am Etude.* Play this song fingerstyle with *free strokes.* It could also be played with a pick. Allow all of the notes to ring (arpeggio style).

Lesson Sixteen

Embellished chords
Am7, Gmaj7, Cmaj7

Drill the Am7, Gmaj7 and Cmaj7 chords (p.40). Students need to memorize which string represents the root of the chord.

Ex. 64

Play ex. 64 with the CD, *Track 41*. The strum on the CD is commonly called the Charleston Strum. The rhythm for this strum is notated in ex. 70 (p. 43).

Notesheet #3
Love Her

Review *G Boogie* and the *Am Etude*. Introduce *Love Her*. It can be played with the CD, *Track 25* or have students play the accompaniment. Create a bass part on the roots of the chords.

Challenge

Add the F#m7b5 to ex. 64. Play the moveable chord forms for the Am7, Gmaj7 and Cmaj7 (p. 61).

Lesson Seventeen

Review

Review ex. 64 with the Charleston Strum. Play *Love Her, Notesheet #3*.

New strum
Latin Strum

Introduce the *Latin Strum*, ex. 65, with the CD, *Track 42* (p.40). This is a new syncopated rhythm. Some students will find the option picking pattern easier.

Songsheet #6
When Johnny Comes Marching Home

Introduce 6/8 time and *When Johnny Comes Marching Home*.

Challenge
improvisation

Continue to work with students who are developing improvised solos using the minor pentatonic scale.

Lesson Eighteen

Review

Review *Celebrate* (p. 83) and *Walking the Bass* (p. 39): achievement standards 15 and 16.

Full Bar F chord
preparation exercise

As preparation for learning how to play the Full Bar F Chord, have the students place the index finger across all of the strings at the 5th fret. The index finger must be *straight* from the knuckle to the tip. Arch the wrist (away from the neck) and place the thumb so that it opposes the index finger. If the right forearm is properly positioned on the edge of the guitar, it will help oppose the index finger. Strum the strings and apply pressure to the outside edge (toward the nut) of the index finger. Drill as follows: strum 4 beats — rest 4 beats — strum 4 beats — rest 4 beats.

Practice

Have the students practice for the playing test. Give extra credit to students who have developed a solo using the D minor pentatonic scale.

Lessons Nineteen and Twenty

Playing Test
achievement standards 14 and 15

Test each student on achievement standards 14 and 15. Give extra credit for improvisation.

Performance Day
sign-up, schedule

As the students are waiting to be tested, they could be preparing for a Performance Day. They need to sign up with you and indicate what they are going to perform, who is going to perform and what equipment they might need (amps, mics, etc.).

Lesson Twenty-One

Performance Day
preparation

You'll need at least a day to coach the performers and allow them time to rehearse. Offer suggestions to the performers. You might participate in some of the performances.

Lesson Twenty-One

Performance Day

Have the students perform for each other. Go over your expectation of the students as a supportive, respectful and attentive audience. They are being evaluated as an audience. You could give extra credit to all of the performers.

Build on the success and motivation students get by preparing a performance. They will be reluctant in the beginning, but if you set the groundwork properly, you will have many students willing to perform. You haven't told them yet, but by the time they get into Unit Six, everyone will be required to perform for the class in a solo or ensemble situation. Take the sting out of this by allowing strong students to play and support the more tentative students. You could also perform with some of the students.

Lesson Twenty-Two

Evaluate Performance Day
plan for the next one

Follow-up and discuss the performance day and make plans for and schedule the next one.

Review

Drill chords and review various songs.

Tabsheet #2

Review the exercises on *Tabsheet #2* and introduce ex. 15. Think of some songs where you could use this accompaniment pattern.

New notation song
Ode to Joy

Introduce *Ode to Joy* (p. 83) with the CD, *Track 73*. Some students might be able to play the accompaniment part.

Lesson Twenty-Three

Review
Unit Test

Lecture, review and assist the students in preparing for the Unit Test. Give them some time to organize their notebooks.

Lesson Twenty-Four

Unit Test

Administer Unit Four Test and collect the notebooks.

UNIT FIVE

Chords & Accompaniment

(pages 41–49)

Music Fundamentals & Theory:
Key of Am, Principal Chords
III and VII Chords in Am
More Embellished Chords

Chords:
Dm, F (small bar)
F (full bar), Dm7
Bm11 (challenge chord)
Dmaj7, D6, A7sus

Accompaniment:
Plucking Pattern in 3/4 (p. 44)
Plucking Pattern in 4/4
Plucking Arpeggio in 4/4
Plucking Arpeggio Variations in 4/4
Plucking Patterns in 3/4 (p. 47)
Arpeggio Pattern in 3/4
Arpeggio Patterns in 4/4
Variations in 4/4

Songs and Progressions:
Ex. 67, Ex. 70 *(Jazz Minor Blues)*
Down In The Valley, Scarborough Fair
Sometimes I Feel Like a Motherless Child
Silent Night, Greensleeves, Ex. 79

Learning to Read Music

(pages 84–89)

Music Fundamentals:
Dynamics
Arpeggio
Flats
Enharmonics
Chromatic Scale
Tied Eighth Note Rhythms
Syncopation

Playing Techniques:
Basic Fingerstyle Hand Position (*plant*)
Free Strokes *(p, i, m, a)*
Right Hand Mute

Notes:
E and F on the 4th string
Review of notes on the 4th string
G# on the 3rd String
Chromatic Scale

Songs:
Andantino, Study
Classical Study
Groovin' (lead), Groovin' (rhythm-bass)

Supplemental Materials

Worksheet
- *#11* Music Writing Practice
- *#12* Enharmonic Notes, Half Steps, Chords, Review

Songsheet
- *#7* Aura Lee, Cruel War

Notesheet
- *#4* Kookaburra (round), Andantino (solo), Arpeggio Study, Theme from Malaguena (high version)
- *#5* Am Study, Riffin' The Blues, Simple Gifts

Tabsheet
- *#2* Exercises 14 and 15

Unit Five Test: Covers the material contained in *Worksheets #6–12*

Lesson One

Key of Am
principal chords

Discuss the Principal Chords in the Key of Am: Am, Dm, and E7 (p. 41). Explain what is meant by *relative minor* and that the Am scale is constructed on the 6th degree of the C major scale. Review Minor Keys (p. 38).

Dm chord

Drill the Dm chord (p. 41). Point out transportation tips. Have the students notice that in the Dm, Am and E7 chords, the 1st and 2nd fingers form the same *shape* and are on the *same* frets (just different strings). Play ex. 66. Memorize the roots of the chords.

Ex. 67

Introduce ex. 67 with the CD, *Track 43*. This chord progression can also be used as an accompaniment to *Friends* notated on *Notesheet #2*. Try playing these two together. Add a bass part.

New notes E and F
4th string

Review the D open 4th string and introduce E and F (p. 84). Play ex. 59–64.

Full Bar F chord
preparation exercise

Repeat the Full Bar F *preparation exercise* described in Unit Four (p.42). Because of the height of the strings at the first fret, do the preparation exercise at the 5th fret. If some of the strings fail to vibrate cleanly, adjust the index finger.

- *over bar:* extend the index finger beyond the neck of the guitar
- *under bar:* adjust the index finger in the opposite direction

You are looking for the "sweet" soft. The index finger needs to be as straight as possible from the tip to the knuckle that joins the hand. And VERY IMPORTANT, the pressure is applied on the *outside* of the index finger. Rotate the index finger toward the nut of the guitar.

Challenge
Improvisation

Have one student play the Dm chord while another improvises on the D minor pentatonic scale.

Lesson Two

Review and assignment
achievement standard 16

Review the principal chords in the Keys of D, G, A, E, Am and Em. In each key, play the I-IV-V7-I or i-iv-V7-i chord progression. Play the root of the chord on the first beat follow by three strums or plucks. Assign for future testing: achievement standard 16.

New notation song
Andantino

Review ex. 67 and the notes on the 4th string (p. 84), ex. 59–64.

Introduce *Andantino* (p. 85) with the CD, *Track 74*. Allow all of the notes in the *solo* to ring (arpeggio style). The accompaniment is a review of the notes on the 4th string. Divide the class, and play both parts.

Challenge
Andantino (solo)

The excerpt of *Andantino* comes from the guitar study by Carcassi. Both parts notated in the book can be played by one guitarist. Pass out *Notesheet #4* and go over *Andantino (solo)*.

Lesson Three

Review the material in the student book regarding the F chord (p. 42). The F chord is difficult for beginners. The simplified fingerings and the Small Bar F are helpful solutions but they don't necessarily build the skills needed to play the Full Bar F chord. Be familiar with the material presented on page 42 of the student book before you present the F chord.

Small Bar F chord

Start with the Small Bar F chord *shape* at the 5th or 7th fret. It is easier to play this chord shape in the higher positions on the guitar (5th fret, 7th fret, etc.), because the strings are closer to the fingerboard and the frets are closer together. The problem occurs with the index finger. It has to depress two strings. The index finger also needs to *rotate* toward the nut so that the pressure is on the *outside* of the finger.

Full Bar F chord
drills

This F chord is sometimes referred to as the E form because it is derived from the open E chord (p. 60). Review the *preparation exercises* previously introduced. Start at the 5th fret and build the full bar chord (also called barre) in three steps.

1 Place the index finger across the strings. When you achieve a good sound, move to the next step.

2 Add the 2nd and 3rd fingers to the chord shape. Keep the index finger straight.

3 Add the 4th finger to complete the formation of the Full Bar F chord.

Finally, remind the students that if the right forearm is on the edge of the guitar, it will act as a counterbalance against the fingers of the left hand and will aid the thumb in depressing the index finger. Circulate around the room to help students.

Ex. 68 and 69

Play ex. 68 and 69. Allow students to use whichever form of the F chord they can handle at this point.

New notation song
Study

Introduce *Study* (p. 85). The accompaniment to this song will provide additional review of the notes on the 4th string. The solo is a good review of the notes on the treble strings.

Lesson Four

Review
F chord

Review the F chord and then play the chord progressions notated in ex. 68 and 69.

Drill the Dm7 chord. It requires the same *small bar* technique used in the F chord. Notice the similarity the Dm7 chord has in *shape* and fret location to the Am7 chord. Practice moving from the Dm7 to the Am7.

New song
Jazz Minor Blues

Play the *Jazz Minor Blues*, ex. 70 (p. 43), with the CD, *Track 44*. The strum rhythm is referred to as the Charleston rhythm.

Challenge

Play the Bm11 in the first ending (turnaround) or play the *Jazz Minor Blues* with moveable chord forms.

Lesson Five

Review	Review the chords and rhythm and then play the *Jazz Minor Blues*.
Worksheet #11	Lecture and demonstrate the material in *Worksheet #11*: Music Writing Practice. Have students complete the assignment in class with your supervision.
Practice	When they have completed the assignment, they should practice for the test: achievement standards 16. Some students may be ready to play the solo version of *Andante:* advanced achievement standard 4.

Lesson Six

Review *chord drills*	Review the I-IV-V7-I and i-iv-V7-i chord drills in preparation for the test: achievement standard 16.
New notation song *Kookaburra*	Introduce *Kookaburra* (round) from *Notesheet # 4*. Start the song in 3rd position.
Challenge *Arpeggio Study*	Introduce *Arpeggio Study* on *Notesheet #4* to those students who have been making good progress on the fingerstyle free stroke techniques.
Practice	Provide time for practice and individual help.

Lessons Seven and Eight

Playing Test *achievement standard 16*	Test the students individually on achievement standard 16. Test any students that may be ready to play the advanced achievement standard 4.

Lesson Nine

The *preparation exercises* presented in the *Tabsheets* should allow the students to move into the Fingerstyle Accompaniment section (p. 44) with ease. Review the right hand playing position. These plucking and arpeggio patterns are played with *free strokes* (called tirando by classical guitarists). Also the Spanish translation for naming the fingers of the right hand are: *p* for pulgar (thumb), *i* for indicio (index finger), *m* for medio (middle finger), and *a* for anular (ring finger).

Fingerstyle *chords and arpeggios*	Review the Basic Fingerstyle Hand Position (p. 86) and demonstrate ex. 65–69 with the CD, *Track 75*. Drill all of the exercises. It is IMPORTANT to establish the *plant* as a preparation position.
Dmaj7, D6 and A7sus chords	Drill the new chords (p. 44): Dmaj7 usually moves to D6; A7sus usually progresses to A7.
New Song *Down in the Valley*	Using the Basic Strum No. 1, play through the chord changes in *Down In The Valley* (p. 44). Practice the Plucking Pattern on open strings and then on the chord progression. Play with the CD, *Track 45*.
Challenge *Theme from Malagueña* *(high version)*	Present the *Theme from Malagueña* (high version) from *Notesheet #4*. The curved line in front of the E chord in measures 1, 11 and 12 means to slowly strum the chord with the thumb.

Lesson Ten

Review
plucking patterns

Review the Plucking Pattern and *Down in the Valley* (p. 44). These patterns could also be play pickstyle.

New song
Scarborough Fair

Introduce *Scarborough Fair* (p. 45). Play through the chord changes, drill the Plucking Pattern on each chord and then play the song. Play the melody on the guitar or piano.

Fingerstyle drills
chords and arpeggios

Play the chord and arpeggio ex. 70–73 (p. 87) with the CD, *Track 76* and then without the CD. Emphasize the need to *plant* the hand in preparation.

New notation song
achievement standard 17

Introduce *Classical Study* (p. 87) with the CD, *Track 77*. Assign for future testing: achievement standard 17.

Challenge
Prelude, Spanish Song

Assign some students to work on the accompaniment parts for *Prelude* (p. 72), *Spanish Song* (p. 80) or *Malaguena* from *Notesheet #4*.

Lesson Eleven

Music fundamentals
flats, enharmonics, chromatic scale

Lecture, discuss and demonstrate the material covered in the student book regarding Flats, Enharmonic Notes and the Chromatic Scale (p. 88). Play ex. 75, the *Chromatic Scale* with the CD, *Track 78*. Discuss the Left-Hand Playing Technique described on this page. Review ex. 75.

Practice

Practice and review songs and accompaniments. Give individual coaching and help to the students who may be struggling. Check how the F chord is developing with individual students.

Lesson Twelve

Plucking Arpeggio Patterns
Sometime I Feel Like a Motherless Child

Introduce the Plucking Arpeggio Patterns (p. 46). Play *Sometimes I Feel Like a Motherless Child* with the CD, *Track 46*. Alternate the thumb (*p*) between the root and fifth of the Em and Am chord. Save *Silent Night* for the holiday season but drill ex. 76 and 77.

Assignment
achievement standard 18

Achievement standard 18 involves playing ex. 2–10 of the fingerstyle accompaniment patterns presented on *Tabsheet #1*: pluck patterns, plucking arpeggios and arpeggios ex. 2–10. The patterns can be performed on any major or minor chord except Em. The thumb (*p*) plucks the root of the chord.

Review

Review the *Classical Study* with the class and *Prelude* and *Spanish Song* with individual students. Also tutor *Theme from Malaguena* (high version).

Lesson Thirteen

Worksheet #12

Discuss and review the material contained in *Worksheet #12*: Enharmonic Notes, Half Steps, Chords, Review. When students have completed the worksheet and turned it in to you, they should practice for the playing test: achievement standard 17.

Practice for Playing Test

Lesson Fourteen

Review
Tabsheet #1, songs

Play ex. 2–10 on *Tabsheet #1* using various chords. For the test, students can play these exercises in quarter note rhythms or as eighth notes. Speed isn't important. Technique, playing position and the resulting sound are important. Review *Scarborough Fair* (p. 45) and *Sometime I Feel Like A Motherless Child* (p. 46). Play the *Classical Study* and the *Chromatic Scale* (pp. 87, 88).

Songsheet #7
Aura Lee

For additional practice playing the Plucking Arpeggio pattern, play *Aura Lee* from *Songsheet #7*.

Challenge
Am Study

The *Am Study* from *Notesheet #5* combines rest stokes (*apoyando*) and free strokes (*tirando*). Students need to *plant* the hand as they prepare to play the root of the chords in the arpeggios.

Lesson Fifteen

Practice and review

Practice and review for the playing test.

Lessons Sixteen and Seventeen

Playing Test
achievement standards 17 and 18

Test students on their ability to play *Classical Study*, fingerstyle accompaniment patterns and other assignments such as the accompaniment to *Prelude* or *Spanish Song*.

Practice

While students are waiting to be tested, they are busy practicing and rehearsing for the next performance day.

Lesson Eighteen

Music fundamentals
tied eighths, syncopation

Lecture and demonstrate the Tied Eighth Note Rhythms and Syncopation presented in the student book (p. 89).

New notation assignment
achievement standard 19

Introduce *Groovin' (lead)* with the CD, *Track 79* (p. 89). The melody is based on the D Blues Scale (see Challenge). Assign *Groovin'* for future testing: achievement standard 19. Play *Groovin' (rhythm-bass)* and review the right hand Mute Technique used to get a "chucking" sound.

Challenge
D Blues Scale

The D Blues Scale adds one additional note to the D minor pentatonic scale which was presented on page 33 of this guide. The additional note is the lowered 5th (b5) or Ab. Create your own solo. Moveable versions of the power chords can be used to accompany *Groovin'*: D5, F5, G5, A5.

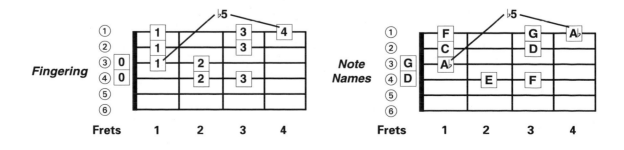

Lesson Nineteen

Review	Review *Groovin'* and the D Blues Scale. Review *Aura Lee* and the *Am Study.*
New song *Greensleeves*	Introduce *Greensleeves* (p. 48) with the CD, *Track 47.* In the second ending and in measure 25, pluck each chord (thumb plucks the root).
Songsheet #7 *Cruel War*	For additional practice performing the Arpeggio Pattern, play *Cruel War* on *Songsheet #7.*

Fingernails

Guitarists use a combination of *flesh* and *fingernail* to produce a tone on the guitar. The fleshy part of the finger pushes or carries the string; the nail quickly passes up and over the string. In general the nails need to follow the shape of your finger tips. Shape the nails with a diamond file (Revlon); avoid crosshatch files. Polish the nails with no. 500 and 600 dry sand paper. In the beginning, keep the nails short but long enough to do the job.

Lesson Twenty

Review	Review *Greensleeves* and *Cruel War.*
New song and assignment *achievement standard 20*	Play the Arpeggio Pattern in 4/4 (p. 49), ex. 78. Introduce ex. 79 with the CD, *Track 48.* Assign ex. 79 for future testing: achievement standard 20.
Notesheet #5 *Riffin' The Blues*	Introduce *Riffin' The Blues* from *Notesheet #5.* It is another example of a solo based on the A minor pentatonic scale. Explain, demonstrate and teach the Triplet rhythm. Triplets were briefly discussed when swing eighths were introduced (p. 22). This song can be played with *Track 30* or with another guitarist.

Lessons Twenty-One and Twenty-Two

Review *Unit Test*	Review music fundamentals and prepare the students for what will be in the Unit Five Test.
Practice and preparation *performance day, playing test*	Provide some time for the students to practice the final playing test of this unit; achievement standards 19 and 20. Coach the students and assist them in rehearsing for the next performance day.

Lessons Twenty-Three and Twenty-Four

Playing Test *achievement standards 19 and 20*	Test the students individually on *Groovin'* (p. 89) and ex. 79 (p. 49). Some students will be ready to play *Am Study:* advanced achievement standard 5. Some students might be able to get extra credit playing some improvised solos. When not being tested, students can prepare for performance day.

Lesson Twenty-Five

Performance Day	Students perform for the class.

Lesson Twenty-Six

Unit Test	Administer Unit Five Test and collect the notebooks.

UNIT SIX

Chords & Accompaniment

(pages 50–61)

Music Fundamentals & Theory
Key of C, Principal Chords and Secondary Chords
I-vi-ii-V7 Chord Progression
Roots and Fifths
Chord Name/Bass Note
Embellishments
Chord Progressions with Bass Line Movement
No root (NR)

Chords:
G7, F (review), Amadd9
Em/D♯, Em/D, Em/C♯
G/B, Am/G, D/C♯, D/B, D/A
Cadd9, C6, Csus
Dm♯7, Dm6, Dmadd9
A7♭9, G7♭9, D7♭9, E7♭9 (challenge chords)
Moveable Chords

Accompaniment:
Alternating Bass/Chord Strum
Syncopated Strum

Songs and Progressions:
Ex. 85, Ex. 86, Ex. 88, Ex 89
Ex. 90, Ex. 91, Ex. 92, Ex. 93

Learning to Read Music

(pages 90–96)

Music Fundamentals:
Dotted Quarter Notes
2/4 Time Signature
A Chromatic Scale
Fermata Sign
First Position (review)
Sharps, Flats and Enharmonic Notes (review)
E Chromatic Scale
G Major Scale (review)

Notes:
A, B, and C on the 5th String
Review of the Notes on the 5th, 4th and 3rd Strings
E, F and G on the 6th String
A Chromatic Scale

Songs:
Gypsy Nights, House Of The Rising Sun
Sleeper's Awake, Blues Rock
Scarborough Fair
House Of The Rising Sun (solo)

Supplemental Materials

Worksheet
• #13 Principal and Secondary Chords, Symbols, Counting, Note Names
• #14 Chord Names, Roots and Fifths, Chromatic Scale, Notes on the Fingerboard

Songsheet
• #8 *Hey Lidee, Goin' Down That Road Feelin' Bad, Freight Train*

Notesheet
• #6 *Dreydl, Dreydl, Old Joe Clark, Theme from Malaguena (low version)*
• #7 *Rocking The Blues, Simple Gifts (solo)*
• #8 *Spanish Theme (practice version), Spanish Theme (solo)*

Moveable Scales
• G Scale, 2nd Position, C Scale, 2nd Position

Unit Six Test: Covers the material contained in *Worksheets #6–14*

Lesson One

Key of C
principal chords

Discuss the Principal Chords in the Key of C: C, F, and G7 (p. 50). The Secondary Chords in a major key are always minor chords. The secondary chords for all guitar friendly keys are on page 58 of the student book. What are the secondary chords in the Keys of G and C?

G7 chord

Drill the G7 chord, ex. 82. Drill the G7 chord moving to the C chord. Notice that these two chords have the same *shape*. The fingers are located on the same frets but different strings. The G7 chord shape could be described as an expanded C chord shape . Review the F chord and then drill ex. 83.

Songsheet #8
Hey Lidee

For additional practice, play *Hey Lidee* from *Songsheet #8*.

Ex. 84 assignment
achievement standard 21

Play ex. 84 and introduce ex. 85 with the CD, *Track 49* (p. 51). Assign ex. 85 for future testing: achievement standard 21.

B and C on the 5th string

Review the A, open 5th string and then introduce the B and C. Play ex. 80–82 (p. 90).

Challenge
moveable chords

Play the moveable chord forms in the Key of C (p. 61).

Lesson Two

Review ex. 85. Drill the principal chords in the Key of C and play *Hey Lidee*. Review the notes on the 5th string (p. 90).

New notation song
Gypsy Nights

Play ex. 83 (p. 91) note review and then introduce *Gypsy Nights* (p. 90). Demonstrate the new note, F# on the 4th string, 4th fret. An alternate fingering is to use the 3rd finger to fret this note. Have the students play both the melody and chords. The song is in the Key of Am (*relative minor*).

Discuss and demonstrate **transposition**. Develop the concept that the principal chords have a relationship to each other that is maintained no matter what the key. Transpose a few simple songs from D to G, from G to A. To simplify the chords and/or to change the range of a song are reasons to transpose. Discuss the Capo and how to use it.

Challenge
Simple Gifts

For additional music practice in reading eighth notes and for preparation to play a solo version of this song, play *Simple Gifts* from *Notesheet #5*.

Lesson Three

Review

Review ex. 81–83 and *Gypsy Nights* (p. 90).

Music fundamentals
dotted quarter notes, 2/4 time

Lecture, discuss and demonstrate the Dotted Quarter Note (p. 91) ex. 84 and 85. Explain the 2/4 time signature.

New notation song
achievement standard 22

Introduce *House of the Rising Sun* (p. 91) with the CD, *Track 80*. In addition to what is suggested in the book, fingerstyle players could also practice using the thumb on all of the notes. Assign this song for future testing: achievement standard 22.

Challenge
House of the Rising Sun (solo)

Some students could go ahead and try the solo version of *House of the Rising Sun* (p. 94). Play the CD, *Track 84*.

Lesson Four

Worksheets #13 and #14
review fundamentals

Review, lecture, demonstrate and discuss the music fundamentals included in *Worksheets #13 and #14*: Principal and Secondary Chords, Roots and Fifths, Chromatic Scale, Notes on the Fingerboard.

Practice

After the students have completed the worksheets, they could practice for the playing test: achievement standards 21 and 22.

Lesson Five

F and G on the 6th string

Review the E, open 6th string and introduce the F and G, ex. 86–88.

New notation song
Sleeper's Awake (theme)

Introduce *Sleeper's Awake (theme)* with the CD, *Track 81*. Have the students play the accompaniment part with the CD or with other students playing the solo.

additional practice songs

For additional practice reading bass notes, play the accompaniment parts for *B-C Mix, Folk Song* and *Ode to Joy*. You need to introduce the F♯, 2nd fret, 6th string to play *B-C Mix* and *Folk Song*.

Notesheet # 6
Dreydl, Dreydl

Play *Dreydl, Dreydl* from *Notesheet #6* for more practice reading the notes on the 4th, 5th and 6th strings.

Challenge
Old Joe Clark

A traditional country style of playing guitar solos is to play the melody on the bass strings with accompaniment chords used to fill in the rhythm. Play *Old Joe Clark*. Use a pick or the thumb to play the melody and strum the chords with the pick or index finger.

Lesson Six

Ex. 86

Introduce the Amadd9 chord (p. 51) and ex. 86.

Review

Review ex. 85 (p. 51) and *House of the Rising Sun* (p. 91).

Practice

Provide time for practicing for the playing test: achievement standards 20 and 21.

Lessons Seven and Eight

Playing Test
achievement standards 21 and 22

Test students individually on achievement standards 21 and 22.

Lesson Nine

Roots and fifths
achievement standard 23

Introduce the Roots and Fifths on all chords (p. 52). Assign for future testing: achievement standard 23. Students need to memorize and play the roots and fifths of all the chords on the Basic Chord Chart (p. 57).

New progression
Ex. 88

Play ex. 88 with the CD, *Track 50* (p. 53).

Review

Review *Sleeper's Awake, Dreydl, Dreydl, Old Joe Clark*.

Challenge
Theme from Malagueña (low version)

Introduce *Theme from Malagueña (low version)* from *Notesheet #6*. Measures 2, 3, 6, and 7 should be played in 2nd position.

Lesson Ten

Review	Drill the roots and fifths on all the basic chords (p. 57) and play ex. 88.
Ex. 89	Introduce and play ex. 89 (p. 53).
Chromatic Scale	Discuss and play the *Chromatic Scale*, ex. 89 (p. 93). Review the left hand *planting* technique (p. 88).
New notation song *Blues Rock*	Play *Blues Rock* with the CD, *Track 82* (p. 93). Students should try to play both the *solo* and the *accompaniment*. Discuss the Fermata Sign.
Challenge *G Blues Scale*	The melody to *Blues Rock* is based on the G Blues Scale. It is similar to the G minor pentatonic scale except that it adds one additional note, the D♭ or lowered 5th. Improvise your own solo based on the G Blues Scale.

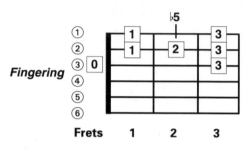 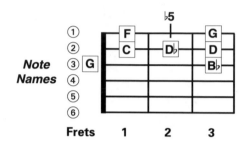

Lesson Eleven

Review	Drill chords, play ex. 88 and 89 (p. 53) and *Blues Rock* (p. 93). Help students develop an improvised solo based on the G Blues Scale.
New chord songs *Goin' Down That Road Feelin'* *Bad, Freight Train*	For additional practice performing chords in the Key of C, play *Goin' Down That Road Feelin' Bad* and *Freight Train* from *Songsheet #8*. Use an Alternating Bass/Chord Strum on both songs.
Challenge	Play moveable chords on the above songs.

Lesson Twelve

Chords with slashes	Introduce chords that include a slash, ex. 90–92 (p. 54). Play the CD, *Tracks 51.1, 51.2* and *51.3*. Play ex. 90.
Review	Review various chord and notation songs.
Challenge *create an accompaniment*	*Peaceful Feeling* (p. 75) has a similar chord progression to ex. 90 (p. 54). Develop an accompaniment for *Peaceful Feeling*.

Lesson Thirteen

New notation song *Rocking The Blues*	Introduce *Rocking The Blues* from *Notesheet # 7*. Review the use of the natural sign and then drill the accompaniment part. Point out the syncopation in measures 2, 4, 6 and 8. There is also syncopation in the *solo* part.
Improvisation *E Blues Scale*	The solo to *Rocking The Blues* is based on the E Blues Scale. Add the lowered 5th to the E minor pentatonic scale to obtain the E Blues Scale; that is, add Bb on the 3rd fret, 3rd string and on the 1st fret, 5th string.

Lesson Fourteen

Worksheet # 14
review fundamentals

Review, lecture and discuss the music fundamentals included in *Worksheet # 14:* Chord Names, Roots and Fifths, Chromatic Scale, Notes on the Fingerboard.

Practice

When the students have completed the worksheet, they should practice for the playing test: achievement standard 23.

Lessons Fifteen and Sixteen

Playing Test
achievement standard 23

Test the students individually on the chord playing tests, roots and fifths on all basic chords. The chords, roots and fifths need to be memorized. Play from memory the I-IV-V7-I chord progression in the keys of D, G, A, E and C and the i-iv-V7-i chord progression in the keys of Am and Em. Also test students who may be able to play any of the advanced achievement standards.

Practice
performance day

When not being tested, students should practice. They could rehearse for the next performance day.

Lesson Seventeen

Review
Rocking The Blues

Review *Rocking The Blues.* Have students form trios; one person on the solo, one person on the written accompaniment, and one person playing a chord accompaniment.

New chords
embellishments

Discuss Chord Embellishments (p. 55). Play the CD, *Track 52* to introduce ex. 93. Drill the C type embellished chords and then the Dm type embellished chords separately. Play ex. 93. Some students could play *First String Warm-Up* from *Notesheet #1.*

New notation song
Scarborough Fair

Introduce *Scarborough Fair,* with the CD, *Track 83* (p. 94). Have the students create their own accompaniment patterns. Add a bass part.

Challenge
Simple Gifts (solo)

Explain and present *Simple Gifts (solo)* from *Notesheet #7.*

Lesson Eighteen

Review

Review chords with slashes and embellished chords. Review and play *Scarborough Fair.* Give individual help to students working on more advanced material.

Notesheet #8
Spanish Theme (practice version)

Review the notes in First Position (p. 95) and then introduce *Spanish Theme (practice version)* from *Notesheet #8.* Practice this song very slowly in "real time." It is a preparation drill for eventually playing the solo version that follows.

Challenge
Spanish Theme (solo)

Some students will be ready to begin practicing *Spanish Theme (solo).* Explain the right hand technique. Have them drill the right hand pattern on the open 1st string and various bass strings before trying to play the written solo.

Lesson Nineteen

Review
Spanish Theme (practice and solo)

Review the notes on the bass strings and play *Spanish Theme (practice version)*. On the open 4th and 1st strings, drill the right hand plucking pattern used in the solo version of this song. Give individual help.

Play songs

Review various songs and advance achievement standards.

Review for Unit Test

Start reviewing what will be included on the Unit Six Test.

Challenge
Moveable scales

Introduce the *Moveable Scales* from the handout: *G Scale, 2nd position* and *C Scale, 2nd position*.

Lesson Twenty

Practice

Provide rehearsal time for a performance day. Tutor the students.

Lessons Twenty-One and Twenty-Two

Performance Day

If you require all the students to perform in one way or another, it will take at least two days to complete the performances.

Lesson Twenty-Three

Review
Unit Test

Review the music fundamentals and prepare the students for Unit Six Test. Have students work on and organize their notebooks.

Lesson Twenty-Four

Unit Test

Administer Unit Six Test and collect the notebooks.

STUDENT SURVEY   Name _____

- What school did you attend last year? _____

- Do you have a guitar ? _____   If yes, what kind of guitar do you have? _____

- List some of your favorite music performers or groups. _____

  _____

- If you have a favorite guitarist, who is it? _____

- Have you ever attended any of the following types of concerts? Please describe and give details.

  Rock, Pop or Jazz concerts _____

  _____

  Musical Theater _____

  _____

  Classical, Symphony, Ballet concerts _____

  _____

- Name your three favorite movies. _____ _____ _____

- Name your two favorite television shows. _____   _____

- Does anyone in your family play a musical instrument or sing in a choir? _____   If yes, please give details.

  _____

- What do you hope to accomplish in this class? _____

  _____

MUSIC PROFILE If you have some guitar experience, have ever played any other musical instrument or have sung in a vocal group of any kind, please answer the following questions. (If you need more room, use the back.)

- What instrument or instruments have you played?   List and give details.

  _____   How long _____ Private lessons? Yes _____ No _____

  _____   How long _____ Private lessons? Yes _____ No _____

- List any private teachers you may have taken lessons from and for how long. _____

  _____

- Do you know how to read music? _____   Do you know how to read tablature? _____

- Regarding the guitar, what chords do you already know? (list) Open string chords _____

  Power chords _____   Moveable or bar chords _____

- What right hand techniques are you familiar with?   Pickstyle _____   Fingerstyle _____

- Have you ever played in a band or orchestra? _____ If yes, please describe and give some details. _____

  _____

- Have you ever sung in a choir at school or in church? If yes, please give details. _____

  _____

- Add any additional information or questions you may have . Use the back if necessary.

COURSE DESCRIPTION — GUITAR I

Prerequisite: You must provide your own guitar. An acoustic guitar is recommended.

COURSE DESCRIPTION
This is an elective course offering beginning instruction for the guitar. You will learn open chords, power chords, moveable chords, accompaniment techniques and a variety of playing techniques and styles including both the pickstyle and fingerstyle approaches to the guitar. The course also includes music fundamentals, theory, songs, performance, listening, composing, improvising, analyzing and learning how to read standard music notation and tablature.

GOALS
1. To learn how to play chords, accompaniment and melodies on the guitar
2. To learn how to read music notation, chord frames and tablature
3. To develop an understanding of music fundamentals and theory
4. To learn how to perform, write and create music
5. To develop the ability to analyze, describe and listen to music
6. To develop the ability to match pitch and sing on pitch
7. To develop an understanding of music as it relates to history and culture

EVALUATION
Grades in this class will be determined on the following basis:
1. Day to day participation, practice, attitude and effort
2. Individual playing and performance tests
3. Group performance tests
4. Successful completion of various Achievement Standards
5. Objective tests on the fundamentals of music
6. Maintaining a notebook
7. Solo and small group performances before the class
8. Working up to your ability — based on the teacher's evaluation of your musical aptitude
9. The school tardy and attendance policy as it pertains to grades

NOTEBOOKS
You will be receiving a number of handouts in this class including worksheets, songsheets, notesheets, tablature lessons, improvisations, scales, chords, etc. Therefore, you must maintain a separate notebook. A three-hole binder is recommended and should be organized as follows:

Course Outline: this page

Assignment Page: to keep track of group and individual assignments

Chords: beginning, intermediate and advanced (moveable forms)

Notation: notesheets, tabsheets and handouts dealing with rhythms, scales, sight reading and ensembles

Songs: songsheets organized numerically and alphabetically

Theory: worksheets and tests

There will be periodic notebook checks. Have your notebook ready for your first check by _____

The **Deadline** for having your guitar in class is _____.

Local music stores that rent guitars or offer the best prices are:

UNIT ONE TEST   **Name** _____ **Date** _____

1.   Name two types of guitars. _____   _____

2.   Which string on the guitar is the lowest sounding string? _____

3.   Write the letter names of the six strings of the guitar.

   6th string _____   5th string _____   4th string _____   3rd string _____   2nd string _____   1st string _____

4.   How many lines are there in a music staff? _____

5.   How many spaces are there in a music staff? _____

6.   The bottom line of the staff is line number _____.

7.   The bottom space of the staff is space number _____.

8.   What is the letter name of line 2 of the treble clef? _____

9.   What are the letter names of the lines of the treble clef, from the bottom up? _____

10. What are the letter names of the spaces of the treble clef, from the bottom up? _____

11. How many letters of the alphabet are used to name notes and the lines and spaces of the staff? _____

12. What do the lines of tablature represent? _____

13. What do the numbers placed on tablature represent? _____

14. Identify the following music symbols.

   a. _____   b. _____   c. _____

   d. _____   e. _____   f. _____

15. Write the letter names of the following notes.

16. Draw stems on the following notes.

17. Write the counting under the notes in the following exercise.

18. Draw the bar lines and add the double bar at the end of the following example.

UNIT TWO TEST   Name _____   Date _____

1. One dotted half note equals _____ quarter notes.

2. One quarter note equals _____ eighth notes.

3. One whole note equals _____ half notes.

4. How many eighth notes can there be in one measure of 4/4 time? _____

5. Music is divided into measures by using _____.

6. What kind of note gets one beat in 3/4 time? _____

7. One half note equals _____ quarter rests.

8. When two dots are placed before a double bar it is called a _____ sign.

9. Tied notes are always on the same _____ or _____.

10. Regarding first and second endings, play the 1st ending, repeat from the beginning, _____ the first ending and play the _____ ending.

11. The distance between two bar lines is called a _____.

12. How many beats will the following notes receive?

    a. 𝅝 _____   b. ♩ _____   c. 𝅗𝅥 _____   d. 𝅗𝅥. _____

13. Name the principal chords in the Key of D: I _____, IV _____, V7 _____.

14. Name the principal chords in the Key of G: I _____, IV _____, V7 _____.

15. The root or primary bass note of the G chord is located on the _____ fret, _____ string.

16. The root or primary bass note of the C chord is located on the _____ fret, _____ string.

17. Numbers placed on tablature indicate _____.

18. Locate the following notes by drawing a circle on or above the guitar chord frame. Write the name under each note.

19. Add the missing bar lines in the following rhythm exercise.

20. Write the counting under each note or rest in the following exercise.

21. Which tempo marking indicates a fast tempo, Andante or Allegro? _____

22. What does Dal Segno mean in music? _____

UNIT THREE TEST   Name _____ Date _____

1. Write the names of the I, IV and V7 chords for the following Keys: Key of D _____ _____ _____ ,

   Key of A _____ _____ _____ , Key of G _____ _____ _____ .

2. In the Key of G, name the chords in the following progression: I _____ vi _____ ii _____ V7 _____ .

3. A sharp (♯) _____ the pitch or sound of a note a _____ step.

4. A curved line used to connect notes on the same line or space is called a _____ .

5. In the following musical alphabet, circle the pairs of letters representing notes that are a half step apart: A B C D E F G A

6 What is the ii chord in the Key of D? _____

7. For notes located below the 3rd line of the staff, the stems go _____ .

8. Compare the two notes in each measure and determine whether the second note is a whole step or a half step lower or higher. Indicate **W** for whole step and an **H** for half step.

9. For each circle or dot on the chord frames, draw the corresponding note on the staff and write its name below the staff. Use whole notes.

10. In the Key of A, write out the proper sequence of chords used in the Basic Blues/Rock Progression.

11. Write the measure numbers in the proper sequence to indicate how the following music would be played.

   a. _____

   b. _____

   c. _____

© 1998 Alfred Publishing Co., Inc. This page authorized for duplication.

UNIT FOUR TEST   Name _____   Date _____

1. To cancel a sharp on any note, use a _____ sign.
2. Lines added above or below the staff are called _____.
3. On which fret is the first finger of the left hand located when you are playing in 2nd position? _____
4. One quarter note equals _____ sixteenth notes.
5. Four sixteenth notes equal _____ eighth notes.
6. Notes added to the basic major and minor triads (three note chords) are called _____.
7. In the Key of Em, the principal chords are _____ _____ _____ .
8. In the Key of E, the principal chords are _____ _____ _____ .
9. How many sixteenth notes can be played on a downbeat? _____
10. What are the names of the open bass strings on the guitar? 6th string _____ 5th string _____ 4th string _____
11. In the following example, write the letter names under the notes.

12. Analyze the music below and answer the following questions: a. How many total measures would be played in this musical example? _____   b. What is the Key Signature? _____   c. What measure is played after measure 4? _____
    d. What is the highest sounding note? _____   e. What is the lowest sounding note? _____

13. In the B7 chord, the root or primary bass is located on the _____ string, _____ fret.
14. Match the music terms with their correct definitions.

    a. _____ tie   1. cancels the a sharp or flat
    b. _____ Dal Segno   2. the ii chord in the Key of G
    c. _____ sharp   3. slow tempo
    d. _____ Andante   4. raises the pitch of a note by one half step
    e. _____ natural sign   5. receive one-fourth of a beat
    f. _____ Am   6. lines added above or below the staff
    g. _____ Da Capo   7. an embellished chord
    h. _____ leger lines   8. receive one-half of a beat
    i. _____ A   9. return to the sign
    j. _____ eighth notes   10. name of the open 5th string
    k _____ Gmaj7   11. the V chord in the Key of G
    l. _____ sixteenth notes   12. return to the beginning of the music
    m. _____ D   13. connects two notes of the same pitch

15. In the following exercises, write the counting under the notes.

UNIT FIVE TEST   Name _____   Date _____

1. Name the principal chords in the Key of Am. _____ _____ _____

2. A flat (♭) _____ the pitch or sound of a note one _____ step.

3. The enharmonic note for: D♯ is _____   B♭ is _____   C♯ is _____   A♭ is _____   F♯ is _____

4. Name two notes that are a half step away from A. _____ _____

5. A natural sign _____ a previous sharp or flat.

6. A chromatic scale is a scale that moves by _____ steps.

7. What are the relative minors to the Key of C _____   and to the Key of G _____ ?

8. Write the names of the notes below and circle the pairs of notes that are a half step apart.

____ ____ ____ ____ ____ ____ ____ ____ ____ ____ ____ ____ ____ ____

9. Match each music term with the correct definition.

a. _____ chord	g. _____ allegro	1. lowers the pitch	7. connects two notes of the same pitch
b. _____ enharmonic	h. _____ tie	2. distance between bar lines	8. divides the staff
c. _____ flat	i. _____ half step	3. loud	9. distance between G and A
d. _____ arpeggio	j. _____ measure	4. distance between E and F	10. pitches sounding separately
e. _____ forte	k. _____ bar lines	5. pitches sounding together	11. raises the pitch
f. _____ sharp	l. _____ whole step	6. fast	12. same sound, different name

10. Under each of the following chords, write an **R** beneath the bass string that represents the root or primary bass note. Write the names of the chords on the lines above each.

a._____   b. _____   c. _____   d. _____   e. _____   f. _____   g. _____

11. On the staff below, write each pitch that is indicated by the chord frame . Use whole notes. Below each note, write their names.

____   ____   ____   ____   ____

12. To demonstrate your music writing skills, copy the following example on the staff below:

UNIT SIX TEST   Name _____ Date _____

1. The dotted quarter note receives _____ beats.

2. The 2/4 time signature organizes the rhythm of the music into _____ per measure.

3. What does a fermata sign (𝄐) indicate? _____

4. In 4/4 time, how many beats would each of the following notes receive? whole note _____   eighth note _____

   dotted half note _____   half note _____   quarter note _____   sixteenth note _____   dotted quarter note _____

5. In the Key of C, identify the following chords: I _____ ii _____ iii _____ IV _____ V7 _____ vi _____

6. In 4/4 time, add the following note values. Your answer may be a number or a note.

   a. ♩ + ♩ = ___   b. ♪ + ♪ = ___   c. ♫ + ♪ = ___   d. ♩. + ♪ = ___   e. ♩ + ♩ = ___   f. ♬ + ♩ = ___

7. Name the principal chords in the following keys: D ___ ___ ___   G ___ ___ ___   E ___ ___ ___

   A ___ ___ ___   Am ___ ___ ___   Em ___ ___ ___   C ___ ___ ___

8. Name the three secondary chords for the following Keys: G ___ ___ ___   C ___ ___ ___

9. Notate the following notes in tablature:

10. Using sharps where needed, write an ascending chromatic scale in whole notes from F to F.

11. Using flats where needed, write a descending chromatic scale in whole notes from G to G.

12. On the frame below, write all of the natural notes and sharp notes.

13. On the frame below, write all of the natural notes and flat notes

Open strings   Frets   1   2   3

Open strings   Frets   1   2   3

SONGSHEET #1

Rock-a My Soul

Moderately

Spiritual

Rock-a my soul in the bos-om of A - bra-ham. Rock-a my soul in the bos-om of A - bra-ham.

Rock-a my soul in the bos-om of A - bra-ham. Oh, rock-a my soul.

So high, you can't get o - ver it. So low, you can't get un - der it.

So wide, you can't get 'round___ it. Oh, rock - a my soul.

Good News

Lively

Spiritual

Good News, char-i-ot's com-in', Good News char-i-ot's com-in', Good

News, char-i-ot's com-in' and I don't want it to leave-a me be-hind.

Alouette

Brightly

French Folk Song

A - lou-et - te, gen-tile A - lou-et - te. A - lou-et - te,

gen-tile plu-me-rai. Je te plu-me-rai la tete. Je te plu-me-rai la tete.

Et la tete, et la tete, A - lou-ette, A - lou-ette, Oh, A - lou-et - te,

gen-tile A - lou-et - te, A - lou-et - te, gen-tile plu-me-rai.

SONGSHEET #2

This Train is Bound for Glory

SONGSHEET #3

Gotta Travel On

Lively   Traditional

Chorus: Done laid a-round, done stayed a-round, this ol'___ town too long,

sum-mer's___ al-most gone, and win-ter's___ com-in' on. Done

laid a-round, and stayed a-round, this ol'___ town too long, and I

feel like I got-ta___ tra-vel on.___

Verses:

    G   **C**   **G**

1. Papa writes to Johnny, Johnny can't come home, summer's almost gone, and winter's comin' on.

    G   **C**   **D⁷**   **G**

   Papa writes to Johnny, Johnny can't come home, for he's been on the chain gang too long. *(Chorus)*

    G   **C**   **G**

2. Wanna see my honey, wanna see her bad, wanna see her bad, yes wanna see her bad.

    G   **C**   **D⁷**   **G**

   Wanna see my honey, wanna see her bad, she's the best gal this poor boy ever had. *(Chorus)*

La Cucaracha

Lively   Mexican Folk Song

La cu-ca-ra-cha,___ La cu-ca-ra-cha,___ Yo no pue-de ca-mi-

nar___ Por-que no tie-ne,___ Por-que no fal-ta___ ci-ga-rri-llos que fu-mar.

En la tie-rra de la rum-ba,___ to-dos sa-ban, to-dos bai-lan___

Es-te bai-le que re-tum-ba,___ Que a-ho-ra va-mos a can-ter.

SONGSHEET #4

Frankie and Johnny

Slowly

Traditional

1. Frank-ie and John-ny were lov-ers,_____ Oh, Lord-y how___ they could love. They swore to be true___ to each oth-er,___ True as the stars a-bove. He was her man, but he was do-ing her wrong.___

Verses:

2. Frankie she was a good woman, as everybody knows. Spent a hundred dollars just to buy her man some clothes. He is her man, but he's doing her wrong.

3. Don't want to tell you no stories. Don't want to tell you no lies. I saw your lover half an hour ago with a gal named Nellie Bly. He is your man, but he is doing you wrong.

Cielito Lindo (Beautiful Heaven)

Moderately

Mexican Folk Song

Pá - ja - ro_____ que a-ban - do - na su___ pri - mer ni - do, su___ pri - mer ni - do, si lo en - cuen - tra o cu - pa - do, cie - li - to lin - do, bien,___ me - re - ci - do.___ I ay, i ay, i ay, i ay,___ Can - ta y no llo - res, Por - que can - tan - do se a - le - gran, Cie - li - to, Lin - do, los___ co - ra - zo - nes.

SONGSHEET #5

SONGSHEET #6

Hava Nagila

Jewish Folk Song

Ha - va na - gi - la ha - va na - gi - la, ha - va na - gi - la ve nis - me - cha.

ve nis - me - cha. Ha - va ne - ra - ne - na, ha - va ne - ra - ne - na,

ha - va ne - ra - ne - na ve nis - me - cha. U - ru u - ru a - chim

u - ru a - chim b' lev sa me - ach, u - ru a - chim b' lev sa me - ach, u - ru a - chim b' lev sa me - ach,

u - ru a - chim b' lev sa - me - ach, u - ru a - chim, u - ru a - chim b' lev sa - me - ach.

When Johnny Comes Marching Home is written in fast **6/8 meter**. There are two beats in each measure; each beat is divided into 3 parts (triplets). Strum two times in each measure.

When Johnny Comes Marching Home

Traditional

When John - ny comes march - ing home a - gain, Hur - rah! Hur -

rah! We'll give him a heart - y wel - come then, Hur - rah!_____ Hur -

rah!_____ The men will cheer, and the boys will shout, the la - dies they____ will

all turn out. And we'll all feel gay when John - ny comes march - ing home._____

SONGSHEET #7

Aura Lee

Slowly   Traditional

As the black-bird in the spring, 'neath the wil-low tree.

Sat and piped I heard him sing, sing of Au-ra Lee.

Au-ra Lee, Au-ra Lee, maid of gold-en hair.

Sun-shine came a-long with thee, and swal-lows in the air.

Cruel War

Slowly   Traditional

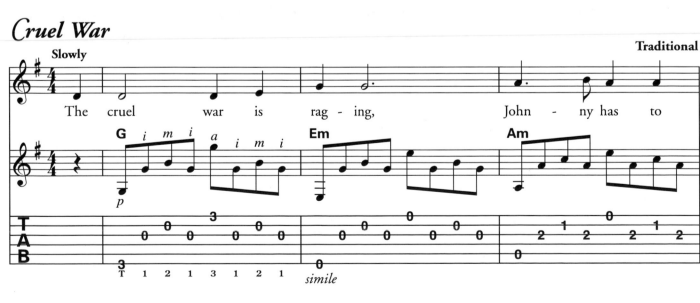

The cruel war is rag-ing, John-ny has to

fight. I want to be with him from morn-ing 'til night.

SONGSHEET #8

NOTESHEET #1

First String Warm-Up Play with *Track 52*, page 55.

Blues/Rock Riff Play with *Track 15*, page 21.

First Duet Play with *Track 16*, page 21.

Easy Does It Play with *Track 21*, page 25.

NOTESHEET #2

Three String Warm-Up

Movin' Play with *Track 22*, page 25.

Friends Play with *Track 43*, page 41.

Jasmine Flower

Chinese Folk Song

NOTESHEET #3

Round

Slowly   Traditional

G Boogie Play with *Track 15*, page 21.

Moderately   J.S.

Am Etude Use free strokes. Let all of the notes ring as in playing arpeggios.

Slowly   J.S.

Love Her Play with *Track 25*, page 27.

NOTESHEET #4

NOTESHEET #5

Am Study Play the melody notes with rest strokes and the arpeggios with free strokes.

Riffin' the Blues Play with *Track 30*, page 30.

Simple Gifts

NOTESHEET #6

Dreydl, Dreydl

Hanukkah Folk Song

Old Joe Clark

In measures 4, 8, 12 and 16, strum the chords from the 4th string.

Traditional

Theme from Malagueña (low version)

Spanish Dance

NOTESHEET #7

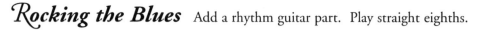

Rocking the Blues Add a rhythm guitar part. Play straight eighths.

NOTESHEET #8

TABSHEET #1

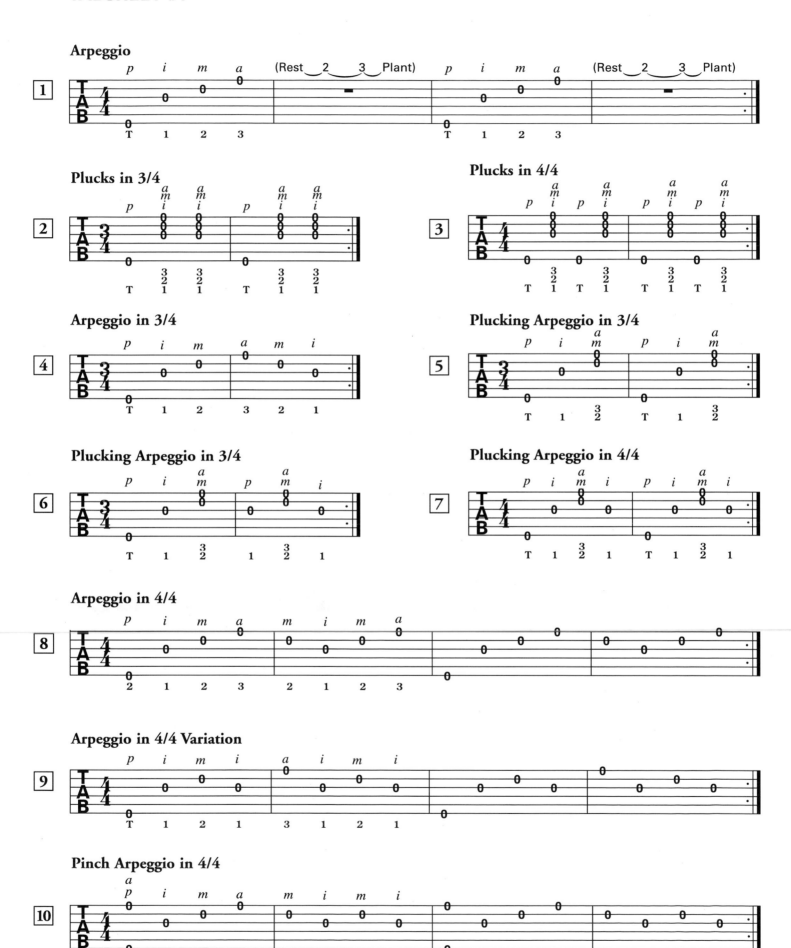

TABSHEET #2

IMPROVISATION SHEET #1

The Improvisation handouts deal with learning how to create or improvise your own solo or lead over a chord progression. The minor pentatonic scale is one of the scales most frequently used in creating a solo on the blues progression. It is a five-note scale that contains the "blue notes" — the lowered or flatted 3rd and 7th. Try playing the *G Minor Pentatonic Solo.* You can play this solo with *Track 15,* page 21.

THE G MINOR PENTATONIC SCALE

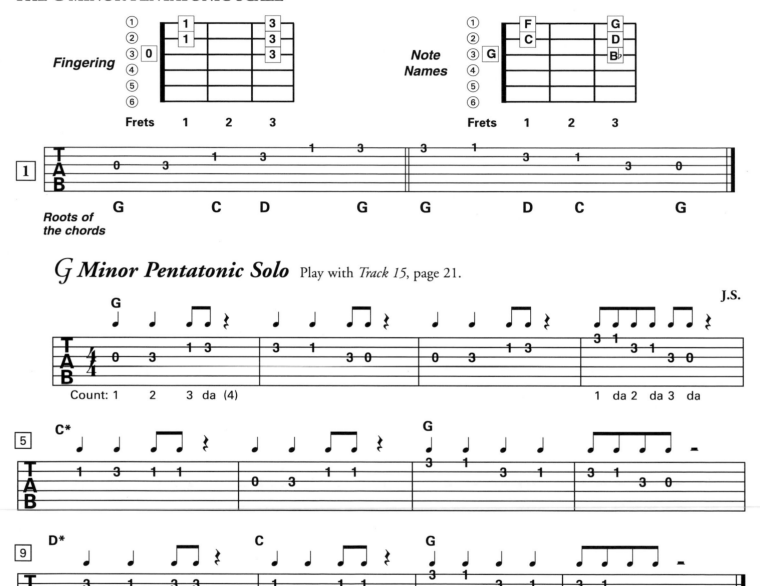

Roots of the chords

G Minor Pentatonic Solo Play with *Track 15,* page 21.

* Optional—substitute C7 and D7.

Challenge

Now try to improvise your own solo. Here are some suggestions:

1. Limit your solo to the first four notes of the scale, that is, the notes on the 3rd and 2nd strings.

2. Memorize the finger patterns and those notes which represent the roots of the G, C and D chords.

3. Use a short rhythmic idea that can be repeated. (Note: these are called RIFFS.)

4. Start and end each riff on the root of the chord.

5. On your first try, only use quarter notes and add eighth note rhythms later.

6. Play your solo with *Track 15* or have another guitarist play the Basic Rock/Blues Progression with you.

7. Try different styles. Rock: play straight eighths; Shuffle and Jazz: play swing eighths.

IMPROVISATION SHEET #2

THE A MINOR PENTATONIC SCALE

The minor pentatonic is a commonly used scale for improvising a melody over the blues progression. It is a five-note scale that contains the flatted third and flatted seventh (the blue notes). The A minor pentatonic scale can be used to solo on the A blues. While you can solo using the entire scale, in the beginning it is better to target the **roots** of the chords and to use and repeat short musical ideas commonly called RIFFS. Try playing the following solo with *Track* 28, page 29. Use this scale to make your own solo.

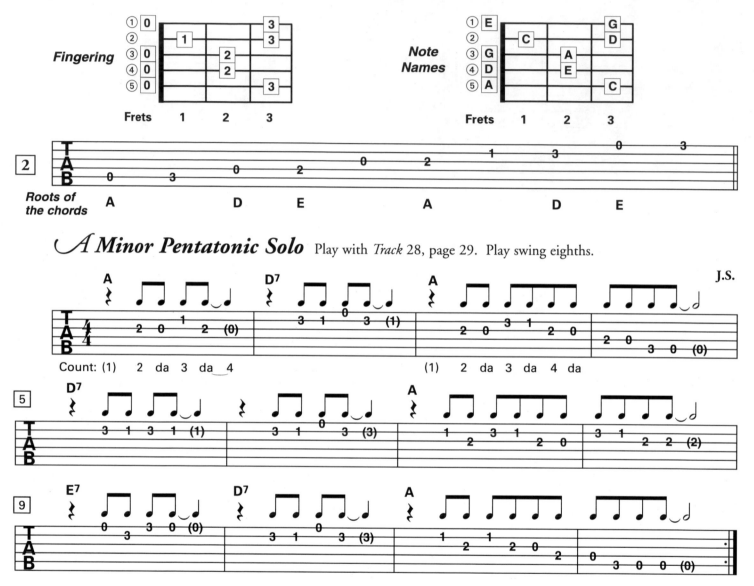

A Minor Pentatonic Solo Play with *Track* 28, page 29. Play swing eighths.

Challenge The following scale is a moveable version of the minor pentatonic. The root of the scale is located on the 5th fret, 6th string. Try creating a solo using this scale. Get accustomed to using the 4th finger. Target the roots of the chords.

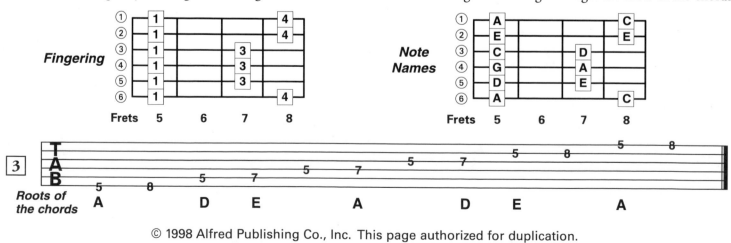

IMPROVISATION SHEET #3

THE E MINOR PENTATONIC SCALE

The E minor Pentatonic scale is a five-note scale which can be used to solo on the E blues. The following solo can be played with *Track* 36, page 35 or with *Track* 33, page 33 or with another guitarist playing rhythm. Try using the scale to improvise your own solo. Start by beginning or ending your riff (short musical idea) on the root of the chord.

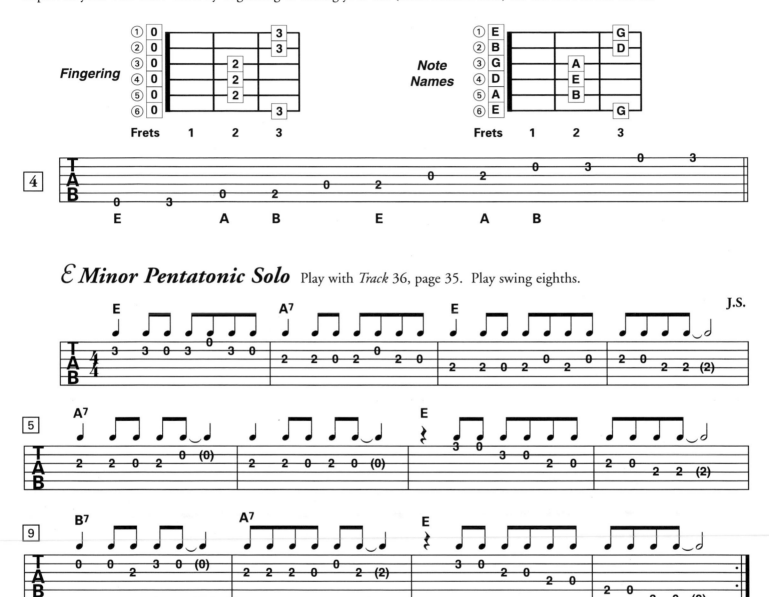

E Minor Pentatonic Solo Play with *Track* 36, page 35. Play swing eighths.

Challenge The moveable version of the E minor pentatonic can also be used to improvise a solo.

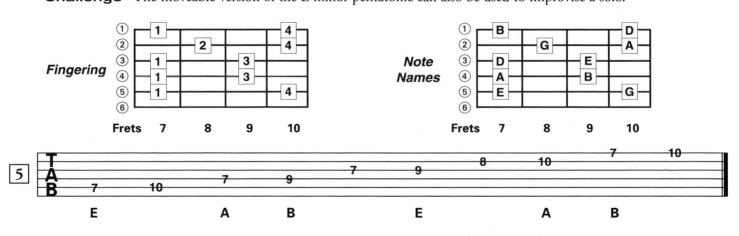

© 1998 Alfred Publishing Co., Inc. This page authorized for duplication.

MOVEABLE SCALES

When you move out of the 1st position, there are many ways to play the major scale on the guitar. The following G and C scales are played in the 2nd position and are often called caged scales. Caged scales are related to and evolve from moveable chord positions. They occur in the span of four or five frets.

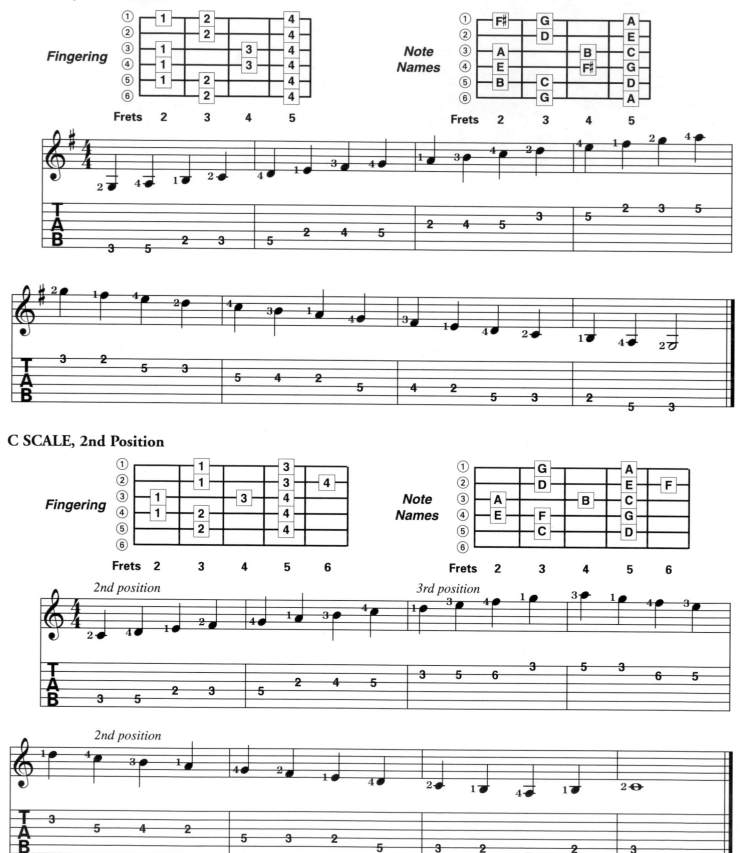

G SCALE, 2nd Position

C SCALE, 2nd Position

WORKSHEET #1

Name _____ **Date** _____

THE GUITAR (Student Book pages 2, 3, 4 and 5)

1. Name four types of guitars. a. _____ b. _____

    c. _____ d. _____

2. What does "action" refer to on the guitar? _____

    _____

3. What is string *gauge?* _____

    _____

4. Match the names of the parts of the guitar with the numbers in the diagram.

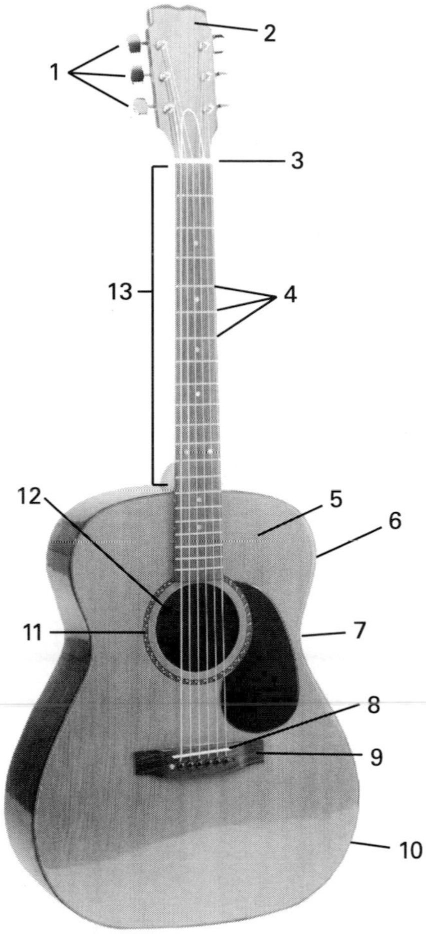

    a. _____ soundhole

    b. _____ fingerboard, neck

    c. _____ rosette

    d. _____ peghead

    e. _____ bridge base

    f. _____ lower bout

    g. _____ nut

    h. _____ frets

    i. _____ tuning keys

    j. _____ bridge bone

    k. _____ top or face

    l. _____ upper bout

    m. _____ waist

5. Which string on the guitar is the lowest sounding string? _____

6. Which string on the guitar is the highest sounding string? _____

7. When you are holding the guitar in the sitting position, which string is closest to the floor? _____

8. When you are holding the guitar in the sitting position, which string is closest to your nose? _____

9. In the spaces provided below, write the letter names of the six strings of the guitar.

    6th string _____ 5th string _____ 4th string _____ 3rd string _____ 2nd string _____ 1st string _____

WORKSHEET #2

Name _____   Date _____

FRAMES, 4/4 TIME SIGNATURE, NOTES, BAR LINES, STAFF (Student Book pages 6 and 7)

1.   Match the numbered parts of the guitar frame with the correct name or description.

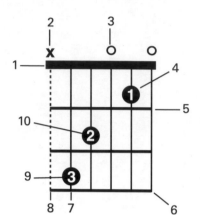

   a. _____   1st string
   b. _____   nut
   c. _____   index finger
   d. _____   1st fret
   e. _____   open string
   f. _____   damp, mute
   g. _____   ring finger
   h. _____   do not include this string
   i. _____   5th string
   j. _____   middle finger

2.   In 4/4 time, how many beats do the following notes receive?

   a. whole note _____   b. quarter note _____   c. half note _____

3.   Identify the following notes:

4.   Assuming the the quarter note receives one beat, add up the number of beats in the following examples:

   a. ♩ + ♩ + ♩ + ♩ = _____   d. o + ♩ + ♩ + ♩ = _____

   b. ♩ + o + ♩ + ♩ = _____   e. ♩ + ♩ + o + ♩ = _____

   c. o + o + ♩ + ♩ = _____   f. ♩ + ♩ + o + ♩ = _____

5.   What does the top number mean in the 4/4 time signature? _____

6.   What does the bottom number mean in the 4/4 time signature? _____

7.   Where is the time signature placed? _____

8.   Bar Lines are used to organize notes into _____ .

9.   A Double Bar is used at the end of a _____ .

10.   What number is the top line of the staff? _____

11.   On the staff, place an X in the following locations:

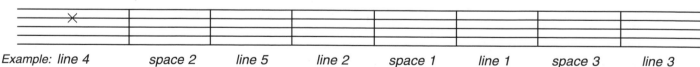

   Example: line 4   space 2   line 5   line 2   space 1   line 1   space 3   line 3

12.   Draw whole notes on the following lines and spaces:

   space 1   line 2   space 4   line 3   space 3   line 5   space 2   line 4

WORKSHEET #3

Name _____   Date _____

TREBLE CLEF, NOTE NAMES, TABLATURE, MEASURES (Student Book page 6 and 7)

1.   The Treble Clef is also called the _____.

2.   Which letters of the alphabet are used to give names to the notes and to the lines and spaces of the staff?

_____

3.   Write the names of the lines of the treble clef from the bottom up.

_____ _____ _____ _____ _____ _____

4.   Write the names of the spaces of the treble clef from the bottom up.

_____ _____ _____ _____

5.   Write the letter names of the following whole notes.

_____   _____   _____   _____   _____   _____

6.   Draw the notes indicated. Use whole notes.

D   G   B   E   C   F

7.   The treble clef is drawn in two steps. Draw four treble clefs.

step 1   *step 2*

8.   Numbers placed on tablature indicate the _____ of the guitar.

9.   A zero placed on any of the lines of tablature means to play _____ .

10.   Which string on the guitar does the bottom line of tablature represent? _____

11.   In the following notation examples, each measure should have four beats. Draw the bar lines and add the double bar line at the end.

a.

b.

12.   How many measures are there in exercise 11a.? _____

WORKSHEET #4

Name _____ Date _____

WRITING and COUNTING MUSIC

A Stem is added to the oval-shaped Half Note and Quarter Note.

For notes located *below* the 3rd line of the staff, the stem is placed on the right side of the note and extends *upward.*

For notes located *on* or *above* the 3rd line of the staff, the stem is placed on the left side of the note and extends *downward.*

The stem needs to be drawn *straight* up or down from the note. The *length* of the stem should extend to the space or line with the same letter name.

In 4/4 time, a Quarter Note (♩) receives 1 beat, a Half Note (♩) receives 2 beats and a Whole Note (o) receives 4 beats. The system for counting rhythms in this book is to use a *curved line* to connect numbers when you want to indicate a contin-

ASSIGNMENT

1, Which direction should the stem go for a 4th space treble clef E? _____

2. Which direction should the stem go for a 2nd line treble clef G? _____

3. Draw stems on the following quarter notes. Write the names of the notes in the space provided.

4. Using half notes, draw the following notes. Do not slant the stems. They need to be drawn straight up and down.

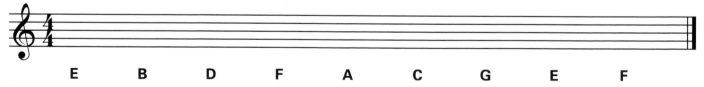

E   B   D   F   A   C   G   E   F

5. In the following exercise, write the counting under the notes. Remember to use a curved line to connect the numbers when counting half and whole notes.

WORKSHEET #5

Name _____ **Date** _____

EIGHTH NOTES, PRIMARY BASS, KEYS, QUARTER REST   (Student Book pages 15–21, page 71)

1. Write in the counting under each slash or note In the following exercises.

2. Which string is the primary bass for the D chord _____, the G chord _____

   and the A7 chord? _____

3. In the Key of G, the principal chords are I _____ ,IV _____ and V7 _____

4. In the Key of D, the principal chords are I _____ ,IV _____ and V7 _____

5. Another name for the I chord is the tonic. What is another name for the IV chord _____and

   the V chord? _____

6. The quarter rest (𝄽) is introduced on page 71. In this book, the system for counting rhythms calls for placing a parenthesis around the numbers under rests. Write the counting under each note in the exercise below.

7. Add the missing bar lines in the following exercises.

8. In the measures below. add the appropriate note or rest above the counting.

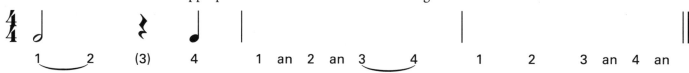

WORKSHEET #6

Name _____ Date _____

TEMPO MARKINGS, REPEAT SIGN, DOTTED HALF NOTE, TIE, COUNTING (Student Book pages 69–73)

1. Match the music terms with the correct definitions.

   a. _____ Quarter Rest   1. Return to the beginning or where there is a double bar line with two dots

   b. _____ Andante   2. Fast tempo

   c. _____ Dal Segno   3. Receives three beats or counts

   d. _____ Repeat Sign   4. Connects notes of the same pitch

   e. _____ Allegro   5. Return to the sign

   f. _____ Dotted Half Note   6. Slow tempo

   g. _____ Moderato   7. Receives one beat or count

   h. _____ Tie   8. Moderate tempo

2. Add the missing bar lines in the following exercises.

3. Write the counting under each note in the following exercises.

4. Add the correct time signatures and write in the bar lines including the double bar at the end.

WORKSHEET #7

Name _____ **Date** _____

REPEAT SIGNS (Student Book pages 24, 25, 71, 72 and 75)

1. How would the following music example be played? Write the measure numbers (1 2 3 4 etc.) in the proper sequence.

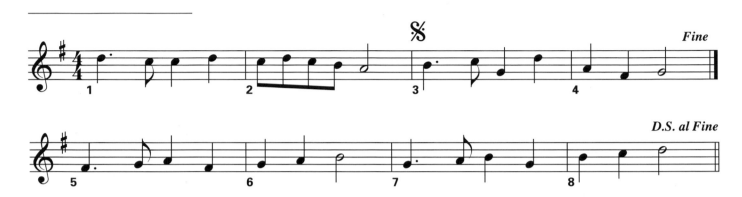

2. Write the measure numbers in the proper sequence to indicate how the following music would be performed.

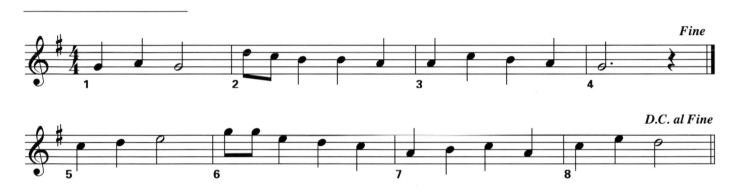

3. Write the measure numbers in the proper sequence to indicate how the following music would be performed.

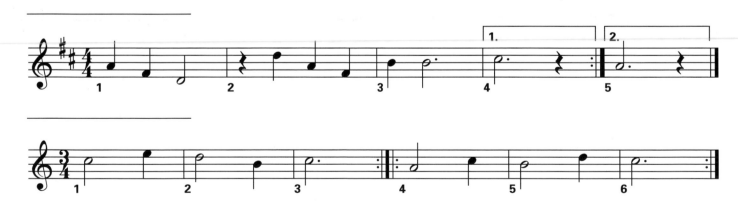

4. Rewrite the following musical example using the first and second endings.

WORKSHEET #8

Name _____ Date _____

NOTES NAMES, CHORD NAMES, ROOTS, PRINCIPAL CHORDS, BLUES/ROCK PROGRESSION
(Student Book review)

1. Write the following notes in tablature.

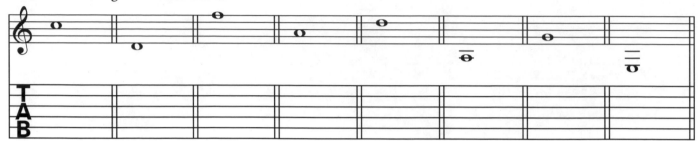

2. Identify the following chords.

a. _____ b. _____ c. _____ d. _____ e. _____ f. _____

3. In the chords above, which bass string represents the ROOT of the chord?

a. _____ b. _____ c. _____ d. _____ e. _____ f. _____

4. Using quarter notes, draw the following notes. Stems need to be straight, the proper length and placed on the correct side of the note.

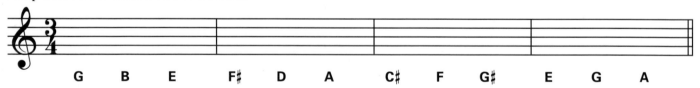

G   B   E   F♯   D   A   C♯   F   G♯   E   G   A

5. In the Key of G, what are the names of the chords used to play the following chord progression?   I _____, vi _____ ii _____ V7 _____

6. In the Key of A, the principal chords are I _____, IV _____ and V7 _____

7. Write the name of the ii chord in the Key of D. _____

8. Write out the proper sequence of chords used In the basic Basic Blues/Rock Progression in the Key of A.

WORKSHEET #9

Name _____ Date _____

HALF and WHOLE STEPS, MAJOR SCALES, MUSIC SYMBOLS (Student Book page 76 and 77)

1. A sharp placed before a note _____ the note one half step.

2. Indicate where the whole steps and half steps occur in the seven letters of the music alphabet (ABCDEFG).
   Use a W for whole step and an H for half step.

   A __W__ B   B _____ C   C _____ D   D _____ E   E _____ F   F _____ G

   Example

3. Compare the first note with the second note in each measure and determine whether the second note is a whole step or a
   half step lower or higher. Use a W for whole step and an H for half step.

   __W__   ____   ____   ____   ____   ____   ____

   Example

4. In the G major scale to the right, CIRCLE
   the pairs of notes which are a half step apart.

1	2	3	4	5	6	7	
G	A	B	C	D	E		F#

5. Match the following music signs and symbols to their definitions.

   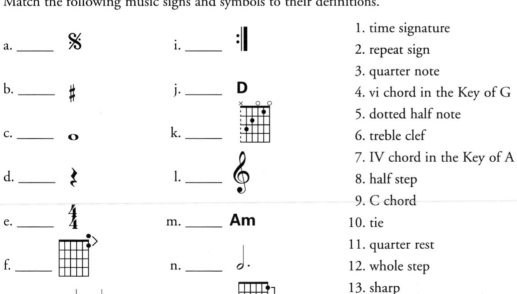

   a. ____ 𝄋   i. ____ :‖

   b. ____ ♯   j. ____ **D**

   c. ____ o   k. ____

   d. ____ 𝄾   l. ____ 𝄞

   e. ____ 4/4   m. ____ **Am**

   f. ____   n. ____ 𝅗𝅥.

   g. ____   h. ____

   h. ____   p. ____ **Em**

   1. time signature
   2. repeat sign
   3. quarter note
   4. vi chord in the Key of G
   5. dotted half note
   6. treble clef
   7. IV chord in the Key of A
   8. half step
   9. C chord
   10. tie
   11. quarter rest
   12. whole step
   13. sharp
   14. dal segno
   15. ii chord in the Key of G
   16. whole rest

6. On the frame to the right,
   write the names of the rectangles.

   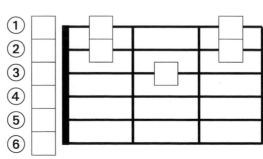

WORKSHEET #10

Name _____ Date _____

PRINCIPAL CHORDS, EMBELLISHMENTS, SYMBOLS, SIXTEENTH NOTES, ANALYSIS
(Student Book various pages)

1. Write in the names of the principal chords (I IV V7 or i iv V7) for the following keys:

   Key of D _____ _____ _____   Key of A _____ _____ _____

   Key of G _____ _____ _____   Key of Em _____ _____ _____

   Key of E _____ _____ _____

2. In the following exercises, write the counting under the notes.

3. What are chord embellishments? _____

4. What Is this sign (♮) called? _____

5. Write the names under the notes in the music example to the right.

6. Lines that are added above or below the staff are _____ _____

7. Analyze the music example below and then answer the following questions:

   a. How many total measures would a musician play ? _____

   b. What is the Key Signature?_____

   c. Name the highest sounding note. _____   d. Name the lowest sounding note. _____

8. Write in the names of the notes and indicate their locations in the frames by drawing in a darkened circle.

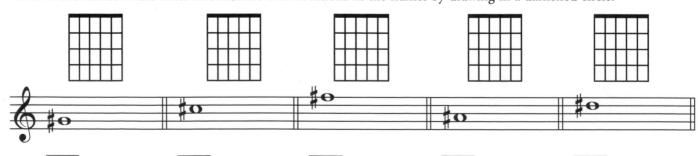

WORKSHEET #11

Name _____ Date _____

MUSIC WRITING PRACTICE

1. Sharps are drawn in two steps:
   a. draw two vertical lines
   b. add two slanted lines

2. A sharp needs to be placed in front of and on the same line or space as the note it is changing.
   Analyze the music example below and then practice drawing sharps in front of each note in the exercise that follows.

3. Flats are drawn in two steps:
   a draw a vertical line
   b. attach a half heart to it

4. A flat is placed in front of and on the same line or space as the note it is changing.
   Study the music example below and then practice drawing flats in front of each note in the exercise that follows.

5. The quarter rest is drawn from the bottom up in four motions. It should be centered on the staff, slightly extending into the first and fourth spaces. Practice drawing quarter rests.

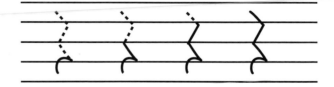

6. In the staff provided, write the following music example.

WORKSHEET #12

Name _____ **Date** _____

ENHARMONIC NOTES, HALF STEPS, CHORDS, REVIEW (Student Book pages 41-49, 84-89)

1. The principal chords in the Key of Am are i _____ , iv _____ and V7 _____.

2. Name three embellished chords. a. _____ b. _____ c. _____

3. Identify the following chords.

    a. _____   b. _____   c. _____   d. _____   e. _____

4. In the chords above, which bass string represents the ROOT of the chord?

    a. _____   b. _____   c. _____   d. _____   e. _____

5. For each of the notes below, write the enharmonic note.

    Example

6. Write the names of the notes below and then CIRCLE the pairs of notes that are a half step apart.

    ___ ___ ___ ___ ___ ___ ___ ___ ___ ___ ___ ___ ___ ___ ___ ___

7. Match the music terms with the correct definitions.

a. ____ piano *(p)*	e. ____ tempo	1. slowly	5. moderately soft
b. ____ mezzo forte *(mf)*	f. ____ allegro	2. loud	6. fast
c. ____ arpeggio	g. ____ andante	3. speed	7. broken chord
d. ____ mezzo piano *(mp)*	h. ____ forte *(f)*	4. soft	8. moderately loud

8. Write the names of the notes in the frames below as follows:

    a. write the sharp names in the rectangles   b. write the flat names in the rectangles

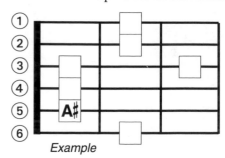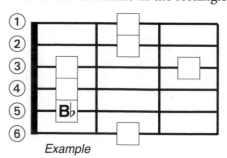

    Example   *Example*

WORKSHEET #13

Name _____ Date _____

PRINCIPAL & SECONDARY CHORDS, SYMBOLS, COUNTING, NOTE NAMES
(Student Book, pages 50–60, 90–96 and review)

1. The principal chords in the Key of C are I _____, IV _____ and V7 _____.

2. Describe what it means when you see a chord symbol such as G/B. _____

3. What does this music symbol (⌢) mean? _____

4. When the normal accent or stress is shifted to a weak beat, it is called _____.

5. In all major keys, the secondary chords are constructed on the 2nd , 3rd and 6th degrees of the major scale.
   Name the secondary chords in the following keys:

   Key of D   ii _____   ii _____   vi _____

   Key of G   ii _____   iii _____   vi _____

   Key of C   ii _____   iii _____   vi _____

6. Identify the following music signs and symbols.

   a. ♯ _____   i. 𝄞 _____

   b. ⌢ _____   j. ♩. _____

   c. ♫ _____   k. *mp* _____

   d. _____   ♮ _____ l. 𝄇

   e. ♭ _____   m. 𝄋 _____

   f. 𝅗𝅥 _____   n. *f* _____

   g. 𝅝 _____   o. 𝄾 _____

   h. 2/4 _____   p. *p i m a* _____

7. Write the counting under the following exercises.

8. Notate the following notes in tablature.

T A B

© 1998 Alfred Publishing Co., Inc. This page authorized for duplication.

WORKSHEET #14

Name _____   Date _____

CHORD NAMES, ROOTS and FIFTHS, CHROMATIC SCALE, NOTES on the FINGERBOARD
(Student Book pages 52, 88, 91, 95–96)

1. Identify the following chords and indicate which bass strings represent the ROOT (R) and FIFTH (5) by writing it below the chord frame (see example).

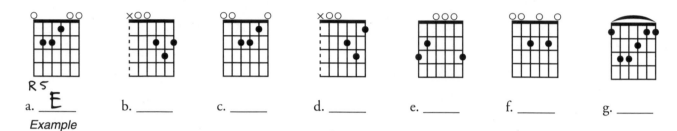

R 5
a. **E** ___   b. ___   c. ___   d. ___   e. ___   f. ___   g. ___
Example

2. Using whole notes and sharps, write an ascending (going up) chromatic scale from G to G. On the second staff write a descending (going down) chromatic scale using whole notes and flats.

3. On the frame below, write in all of the note names. On the frets that contain both sharps and flats, put the sharp name to the left followed by the flat name (see example).

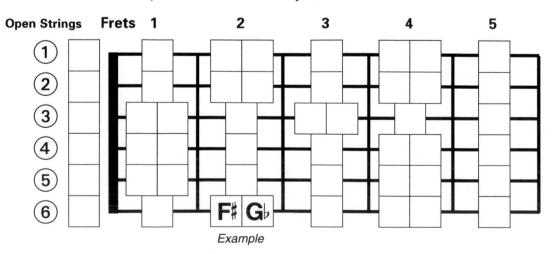

Example

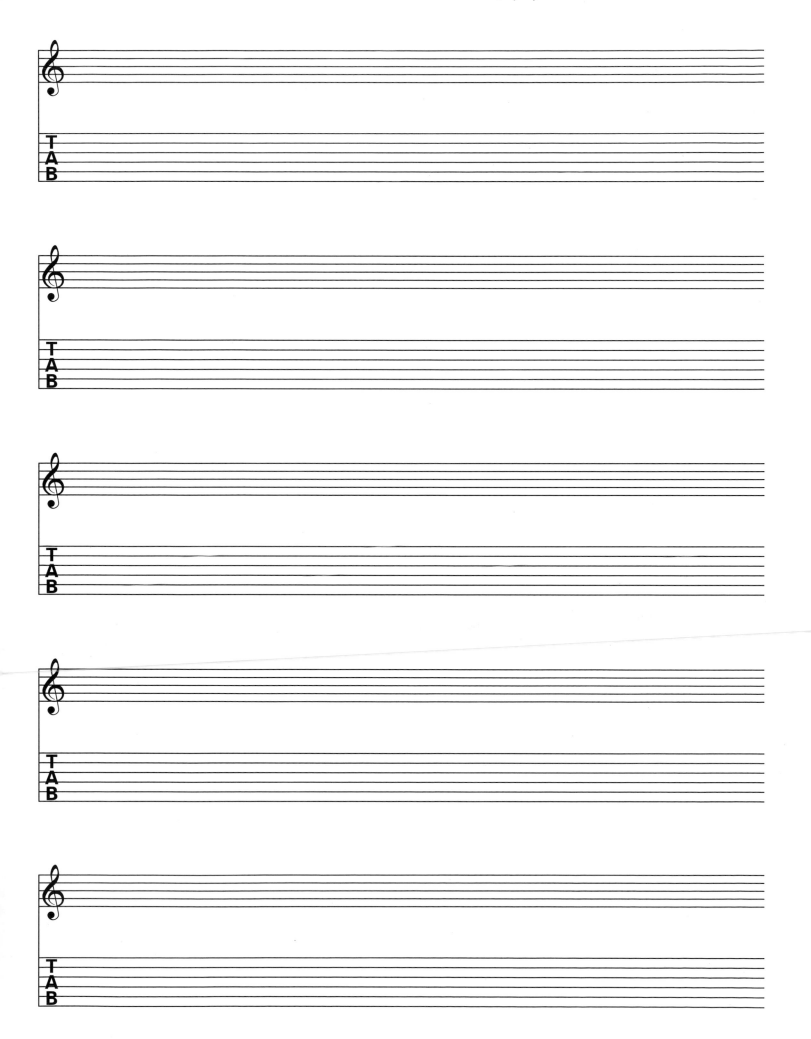

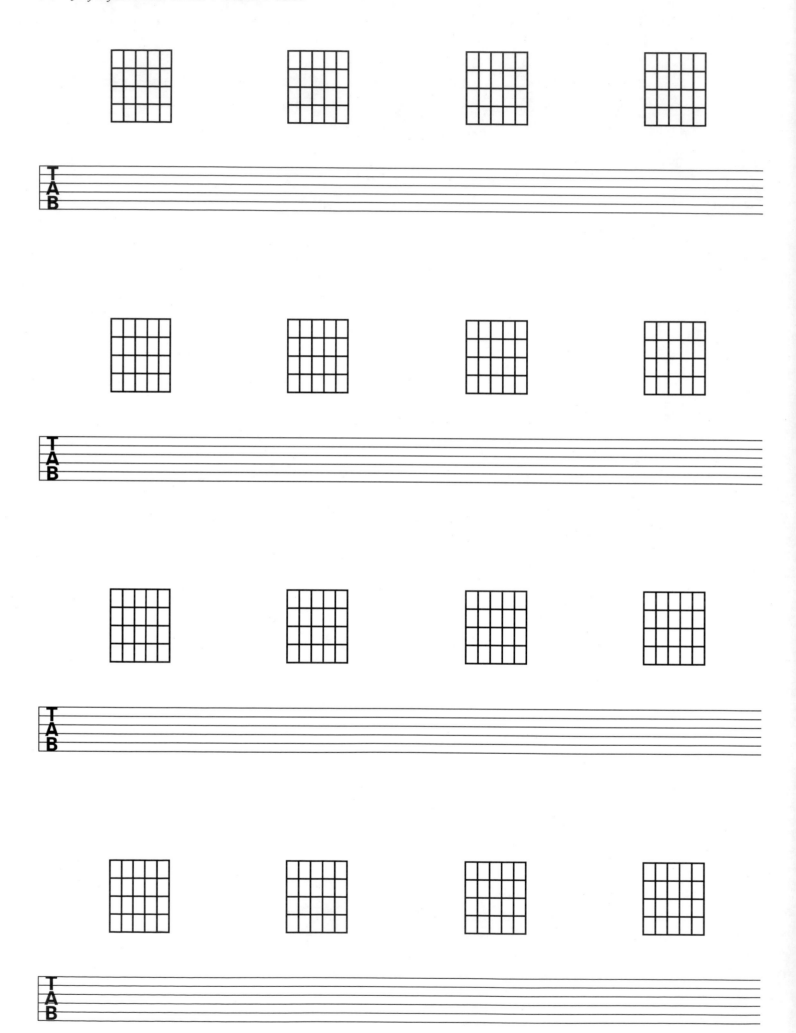